P9-DZN-411

Also by Lawrence Scanlan

Big Ben

Grace Under Fire:
The State of Our Sweet and Savage Game

Heading Home:
On Starting a New Life in a Country Place

Horses Forever

Little Horse of Iron:
A Quest for the Canadian Horse

The Man Who Listens to Horses
(with Monty Roberts)

Riding High:
Ian Millar's World of Show Jumping
(with Ian Millar)

Wild About Horses:
Our Timeless Passion for the Horse

HARVEST OF A QUIET EYE

– the cabin as sanctuary –

LAWRENCE SCANLAN

VIKING CANADA
Penguin Group (Canada), a division of Pearson Penguin Canada Inc.,
10 Alcorn Avenue, Toronto, Ontario M4V 3B2

Penguin Group (U.K.), 80 Strand, London WC2R 0RL, England
Penguin Group (U.S.), 375 Hudson Street, New York, New York 10014, U.S.A.
Penguin Group (Australia) Inc., 250 Camberwell Road, Camberwell, Victoria 3124, Australia
Penguin Group (Ireland), 25 St. Stephen's Green, Dublin 2, Ireland
Penguin Books India (P) Ltd, 11, Community Centre, Panchsheel Park,
New Delhi – 110 017, India
Penguin Group (New Zealand), cnr Rosedale and Airborne Roads, Albany, Auckland 1310,
New Zealand
Penguin Books (South Africa) (Pty) Ltd, 24 Sturdee Avenue, Rosebank 2196, South Africa

Penguin Group, Registered Offices: 80 Strand, London WC2R 0RL, England

First published 2004

1 2 3 4 5 6 7 8 9 10 (FR)

Manufactured in Canada.

NATIONAL LIBRARY OF CANADA CATALOGUING IN PUBLICATION

Scanlan, Lawrence
Harvest of a quiet eye : the cabin as sanctuary / Lawrence Scanlan.

Includes bibliographical references.
ISBN 0-670-04452-0

1. Log cabins. 2. Solitude. 3. Philosophy of nature.
4. Scanlan, Lawrence—Homes and haunts. I. Title.

TH4840.S32 2004 646.7 C2004-901248-7

Visit the Penguin Group (Canada) website at **www.penguin.ca**

For Michael Keeling

and for every labourer
—skilled and otherwise—
who helped recast the cabin

Contents

INTRODUCTION

One evening in the spring of 2002, I found myself talking with Peter and Nicole, fellow dinner guests, about a book I had in mind—on our need for sanctuary, for quiet time in nature, the salve of solitude. And I was overjoyed to hear that these two people, virtual strangers, were completely in sync with me. It was as if I had plucked from my pocket a smooth round stone—something I rubbed for good luck—and they each responded, first by admiring it, and then by reaching into their pockets and producing their own smooth round stones.

Peter once had a cabin in the woods and, though he had to give it up, he spoke of it like someone recalling a beloved grandmother who had pampered him as a child or a cherished pet long gone but fondly remembered. Nicole, similarly, every year rents a cabin on a lake deep in late autumn when the place seems hers alone. She goes there with only her dog as company, a pile of books, and an eye and ear open.

William Thorsell, the former editor-in-chief of the *Globe and Mail,* would have been a keen addition to that dinner table as we compared our smooth round stones. Just days earlier, his old newspaper had run a piece on Thorsell's retreat—a relocated barn on a patch of land north of Toronto. Thorsell had bought the fifty-acre piece five years previously and got the feel of it by bunking in an old plywood cabin on the side of a hill. What nurtures him now are the panoramic views of storms rolling in from afar, the changing palette of the fields through the seasons, the arrival of birds in the spring and their departure in the fall. Some nights he will take a flashlight into the woods and turn off the beam to take in all that's unfolding in the darkness.

Rachel Carson, on the other hand, used the flashlight as a teacher uses chalk. In the last book she wrote, in 1964, she describes taking her young nephew into the fields after dark to find crickets, "for an hour of hunting out the small musicians by flashlight is an adventure any child would love. It gives him a sense of the night's mystery and beauty, and of how alive it is with watchful eyes and little, waiting forms." In that book, *The Sense of Wonder,* Carson urges us to go beyond the naked eye, to use both the wide lens and the close-up. Without a magnifying glass, she says, we would miss the "exquisite handiwork" of a snowflake. The photograph of herself she liked most shows her leaning against a tree in the woods of Maine, a set of binoculars on a strap over her shoulder.

"Theatre," Thorsell calls what happens on his land, then adds, "What is happening outside is the show and everywhere the seats are good." In that *Globe* article, Thorsell argues that the land, "wild land," he calls it—for it comprises high meadow, steep ravine, and dense forest—is his own prescription for good health. He believes that clearing paths, chopping wood, and putting his shoulder into boulders all steel the body in a way that exercise gyms cannot. "Nature," Thorsell insists, "is a dominatrix, and very good for your heart and corpus." Up there he feels deeply connected to that land, the community, the earth itself. The prospect of endless projects—a bridge over the creek here, a sculpture in the grove over there, orchards everywhere—delights him to the core of his being.

Books such as Annie Dillard's *Pilgrim at Tinker Creek* and E.O. Wilson's *Biophilia* belong in both Thorsell's fancy barn and my own rustic cabin in southeastern Ontario. Alive to creation and the art of seeing, they are books I read long ago and keep coming back to. Along with a great many others, Dillard and Wilson embrace the old notion that God or spirits infuse the trees and creatures, that the sun setting on waters is somehow holy.

Old notion indeed. Some of the first temples of the first peoples of the world—the eighteen-thousand-year-old cave paintings at Lascaux in southern France, for example—seemed to pay homage to the animals of the day. Even to stand in the precise replica cave at Lascaux (the original has been closed to safeguard it from pollution), to see those ochre and black bison, deer, and horses galloping on those torchlit walls and ceilings, was for me as intensely spiritual as gazing at the Sistine Chapel in Rome twenty-five years before. The Greek philosopher Xenophanes formulated ideas on the blessedness of nature more than five hundred years before the birth of Christ, and the Italian philosopher Giordano

Bruno was burned at the stake in 1600 for daring to suggest that everything was alive and one and that God was part and parcel of the fields and trees, the mountains and seas. Indeed, his executioners had clamped a torture device to his tongue lest he voice that heresy as he died.

I have remarked to others on the deep sense of peace I can feel at the cabin while listening to jazz, how the music swirls around those big timbers like incense in a cathedral, and how taken aback I am that a modest cabin in a field can be so divine.

The cabin makes a virtue of *s*-words, such as *simplicity* and *solitude* and *sanctuary*. At the cabin, instinct often prevails over reason, old over new, the nineteenth century over the twentieth, quiet over noise (I took in a free fridge from my mother-in-law only after first ensuring that its low hum posed no threat to the cabin's utter quiet. Even so, I sometimes unplug the old Admiral in the evening lest it sully the Balkan choir of crickets). Call me a contrarian, but the cabin brings me a little of what I call, with some trepidation, contentment. That's a dangerous word, one that sounds almost boastful, like a prescription for happiness.

What is it about this setting that triggers in me a spiritual calm, the kind I used to feel as an altar boy and have not felt in decades? Is it not to be trusted? Is it as much about absence (no phone, obligations suspended) as it is about presence (birdsong, open fields, sustaining rituals)? Or is it something as simple as this: cabin, land, and quiet all conspire to let the world in, and the world at the cabin is the world of nature.

You will remember the Agence France-Presse photograph that came to symbolize the events of September 11, 2001. A dust-caked man in a suit grimly pressing on while clutching a briefcase in his left hand, his right hand holding a paper towel over his mouth and nose. The photo was reprinted all over the world, including on the cover of *Fortune* magazine. The man, it turns out, was a fifty-nine-year-old entrepreneur named Ed Fine who was on the seventy-eighth floor of the World Trade Center's North Tower when the plane hit. His escape was a miracle. That night, as he was making ready to retire for bed at his home in North Plainfield, New Jersey, he looked out his window and saw a deer lying on his lawn. The big antlered buck turned and stared at him. "It was like I was looking into God's eyes," Fine later observed during an interview with the *Globe and Mail*. "And he was looking into my soul. He was saying to me, 'If you thought you were alone, you weren't. I was with you every step of the way.'" This from a man whose spiritual sensibilities had dulled over time. I took him to mean that there was comfort in that contact with a wild creature, that the experience was all at once calming, reassuring, and strangely meaningful.

For years, a toad almost the size of a grapefruit lived in the grass on the north side of my cabin, and, when he finally disappeared, I missed him, missed chatting him up, missed his fat and lordly manner. The forest across the road is on the flight path of several great blue herons, and their coming and going at virtually the same moment at dawn and dusk seem to provide a truer sense of time than that from a watch. The red-tailed hawks in our forest that complain and take flight when I walk within sight of their nests, the deer that stare back haughtily before bounding gracefully away, the praying mantises to be found easily and everywhere in the high grass around the cabin—all seem part of the place, its essential web and weave.

In May, trilliums—thousands of them, in a great circle and impeccably white, as if snow had piled there and defied melting—rise up from the forest floor at the north end of the acreage. In that dappled spring shade, before the trees all leaf out, the wildflowers are quiet glories and I knew the first time I saw them—and took solace in the thought—that as long as I lived and long after, that sea of trilliums would return. Next spring, and the next, on and on. It seemed terribly important that I have such a place to go to, a retreat, a sanctuary. Did others also feel it?

Certainly many others I talked to or read about while researching this book—men and women present and past, coast to coast, with their own shacks and cabins and safe havens on treasured land—feel the same sense of kinship. In her recent book *Starting Out in the Afternoon: A Mid-Life Journey into Wild Land* (a first book that was also nominated for a Governor General's Award), Jill Frayne embraces a wider notion of land loved. In her case, it wasn't a specific piece of wilderness, but wild land from Ontario to the Yukon, and solitude, that rescued her from her doldrums. She writes about opening her skin to the land, pressing her ribs into the moss, taking warmth from the stones: "It is union with an overpowering lover, no different, I think, from the experience of being in love."

I remembered reading about New Yorkers, in the wake of September 11, fleeing the city as the citizens of Pompeii fled Vesuvius. The residents of Manhattan weren't just escaping the toxic fumes, the anguish, and their own sense of disbelief. They were heeding a deeply felt instinct to shed what Annie Dillard calls "life's noise," which had suddenly hit the pitch of a scream. Many New Yorkers walked in the woods, sat by streams, found peace at lakeside inns and lodges in the Adirondacks. Many who stayed in Manhattan (its pet emporiums would later report) bought songbirds for their dust-plagued digs. What I observed was an overwhelming need for sanctuary, and the certainty—on the part of many—that quiet time in nature, or, failing that, at least some contact with nature, would offer it.

What took shape was a book that would explore the idea of sanctuary, and, to illustrate, *my* sanctuary—a simple nineteenth-century log cabin that I helped rebuild on my family's small acreage. The plan was to take a pioneer's home first built in 1827 and restore its dignity. Owing to my woeful inexperience as builder and contractor, the actual recasting of those timbers was marked by a series of calamities that seemed near tragic as they struck. But in the way that hitting one's thumb with a hammer can evolve with time from lamentable to laughable, my follies as carpenter's apprentice and besieged overseer now mostly amuse.

This book, in part, chronicles the building of my cabin (which my wife, Ulrike, still calls "Larry's Folly" for all the woe and dough that its construction exacted). My dreamy retreat went off the rails early. The backhoe guy made the hole for the foundation too small; we had to bring in a rock-crunching, bank account–swallowing digger the size of a T. Rex. The stonemason, though gifted, was hopelessly late and threw the summer schedule out of whack. My log man fought with the building inspector, leaving me to pick up the pieces. Chinking in November wreaked havoc with the curing process of the cement and led to leaks—many, many leaks—the following spring. One entire wall, the south wall, had to be redone. The log guy blamed the chinker; the chinker blamed the logs; I blamed my foolish heart.

For all that, and likely because of all that, my feeling for the place—a getaway I typically get to one or two days a week, longer in summer—has grown ever deeper. "Harvest of a quiet eye" is a line from the William Wordsworth poem "A Poet's Epitaph," written in 1799. The thirteenth stanza reads: "In common things that round us lie/Some random truths he can impart,—/The harvest of a quiet eye/That broods and sleeps on his own heart."

For most of his life, Wordsworth was a pantheist—as I think I am—who was sustained and inspired by time, and especially time alone, in nature. I read somewhere that Wordsworth walked an estimated one hundred and eighty-six thousand miles in his lifetime.

Wordsworth, Emerson, Thoreau, and Whitman in the nineteenth century, Annie Dillard, E.B. White, Barry Lopez, and Wendell Berry in the twentieth, E.O. Wilson in the twenty-first—all have sung that song of the earth, now sweet, now sad, now cerebral, but always full of wonder. The melody is still resonant, today more than ever. E.O. Wilson—the distinguished entomologist and world authority on ants and twice winner of the Pulitzer Prize (he alone holds that distinction)—has argued that human salvation lies in our fascination for life. Our old instinct to tame nature by making war on it ("Nature, red in tooth and claw," Tennyson wrote in "In Memoriam") is giving way to another instinct that finds deep satisfaction in observing and understanding nature. "Our existence," Wilson writes in *Biophilia*, "depends on this propensity, our spirit is woven from it, hope rises on its currents."

I knew that to be true, but my grasp of that truth was more rooted in principle than real. The cabin brought it home, for the cabin would become my retreat: my place to saunter in the woods with my dog, admire the setting sun, stare into evening fires, watch for shooting stars from the hammock, sit in my rocker and read. At the cabin I breathe deeply, pause mightily, putter away with hammer and saw. The sense of peace available there is nowhere else to be found.

In 1954 when he penned his essay "A Slight Sound at Evening," in praise of the book that Henry David Thoreau had written on Walden Pond precisely a century before, E.B. White was more or less my age, give or take an ache or two. He was arguing then that "if our colleges and universities were alert, they'd give a cheap pocket edition of [*Walden, or, Life in the Woods*] to every graduating senior." Thoreau went to the woods to report on the news from the woods; but he also went for a simpler reason. "At a certain season of our life," he wrote in Walden, "we are accustomed to consider every spot as the possible site of a house."

Whatever instinct propelled me to raise those old timbers in the middle of a field got me into a mess of trouble and levied no small tribute in grief before the cabin became what it is now: a place to hear that old song of the earth.

In the pages to follow, I look at the log cabin in North American history and literature and seek to explain how this sort of retreat can keep us grounded by its elemental pleasures. Thus the book's four chapter headings: Earth, Fire, Water, Wind. Each chapter takes a little trip, but never too far from the hand-hewn timbers that have sheltered—in turn since 1827—a pioneer family, their hired hands, swine and fowl, and finally, me and mine.

No structure conveys more powerfully the pioneer dream than the log cabin. This book on one such cabin is by turns personal and practical, with dollops of history and philosophy and ecology. This is a book about my own dreams—and nightmares. This is also a book about retreat—and the price to be paid (I well remember how the bills for labour and materials came on like a hailstorm in June). This is a book about an amateur in over his head, about things going wrong, horribly wrong. Some tradespeople deceive and fail to please or even to show. At times I felt like an actor in a bad film—the carpenter's goofy apprentice woefully miscast as foreman—and the whole process threatens to unravel, taking me with it.

I will not dwell on tangled specifics of the cabin's construction, as a *Fine Homebuilding* writer might, but on the broad strokes. I'm more interested in emotional physics than the other kind, though both have a place here. My hope for the book is that the reader might be compelled to try building something similar, while avoiding my mistakes. Perhaps readers will want to borrow a friend's cabin and try it for a weekend, or simply walk a friend's land. Even the armchair hiker may find some pleasure in my walks through the fields, my forays to a nearby point of land that juts out into a great lake, and in the sometimes tortuous, sometimes comic journey that brought Anna Bresee's pig barn in pieces to my little field.

earth

A few summers back, I engaged in a rescue: the plucking of a pioneer log cabin from the farm north of Kingston where it had stood since 1827, its dismantling and transport on a flat-bed truck, and its rebirth on our modest acreage in Prince Edward County. The breathing of new life into that plain square-timbered cabin seemed a tortured enterprise at the time, for the rebirth was charged with labour pains. But that cabin would become my own small glory.

I often go there alone, though not really alone, for Dusty comes with me. A golden mélange of husky, border collie, and terrier rescued as a pup from an animal shelter in Napanee, she is now closing in on the stately age of eight. Dusty commences to whine and cry, cry in an anguished, heartfelt way, at the first sign of me packing the truck for the cabin. *Please* take me, she begs, *please please please.* Huskies are among the most vocal of dogs, while border collies may be the brightest and terriers the most determined, and I contend that it is the husky in Dusty that gets her pleading, the border collie blood that bids her plot strategy, the terrier genes that fuel her persistence. To spare household ears, I have tried to mask my preparations for leave-taking, shutting doors so that she can't observe the easy clues—the schlepping of portable CD player, small cooler, black weekend bag, hefty bottles of water. But I must emit a particular pheromone that lets Dusty know that the cabin is in the offing, or perhaps my footfall on the stairs changes, becomes lighter and quicker and gives me away. There is no fooling her.

So I park her in the front seat of the truck and continue loading. Once at the cabin, Dusty will make for the high grass, roll her back into it, dog-paddle in the air, and in every way proclaim her pure joy at being there. More muted but no less keen, I just take a deep breath and smile every time I drive that long gravel lane leading to the cabin. In the way that lovers sup on the mere sight of the beloved, I find pleasure and relief in simply seeing it again, in knowing that it's still there and intact. In our affection for the place, Dusty and I are as one.

When the *Ottawa Citizen* published in its weekend magazine my piece on the building of the cabin, the article was called, simply, "Larry's Folly," and a clever editor added this subhead: "A square-timbered cabin that sits firmly between heaven and hell."

What seemed a leisurely project in spring spilled into haste in summer and an all-out sprint in fall to get the thing (as in the *damn* thing) closed in, roofed in, boarded up—before the snow flew. Most mornings that year I was on the job site, an hour and a half from home, and most evenings back home on the phone, seeing to the next, always tangled, phase. I consulted friends and authorities and tradespeople close to home, along with my uncle, the erstwhile building inspector in northern Ontario. I made decisions by the hundreds: excavation, foundation, insulation, ventilation, regulation … tribulation. I was unnerved and consumed. Ulrike had it right. Fool. Foiled. Folly.

For each phase of construction I created file folders—they sit in a cardboard box in a long and low bedroom closet at the cabin, though I can barely bring myself to look at them. There's a Foundation file, a Roofing file, one marked Tool Shed, others that say Plans, Electrical, Insulation, Windows, Mortgage … One called Budget I find darkly amusing. By far the thickest, and least amusing, is one simply called Bills. One sad little file is called Kurt's Cabin: I had this notion of building my then ten-year-old son a playhouse in the woods, and he even drew up plans and sketched in where he thought bunk beds, dressers, and toy box should go. Never built. (With luck I'll build it for my grandchildren.)

In the box are letters to tradespeople, and they range from formal to friendly, handwritten to typed, from pleasant notes of inquiry to mildly menacing dispatches from the several fronts of some small private war. Some notes still give off a whiff of pure exasperation, like the one to the stonemason—which he duly signed—declaring that if the fireplace and chimney work were not complete by a certain date, a penalty of 2 per cent a day of the total cost of the project would be "inflicted" until the job was complete. The job, of course, was horribly late—like the foundation job that had preceded it and led to my stiff and solemn legalese. Still, I was a soft (-hearted? -headed?) contractor with no stomach for levying the fine the contract called for. Had I done so, the fireplace that was so late in coming would have come at no cost to me.

The mason seemed to live hand to mouth and while *he* was ever tardy *I* couldn't write his cheques fast enough. "I have to feed my kids," he'd say, both proud and pleading, and perhaps he was telling the truth. Or perhaps he was like the Gypsies I saw in southern Spain amusing themselves in the evening by tying thread to a wallet, laying it in the gutter and then pulling it ahead a few inches when someone (me, for instance) reached for the bait. I remember feeling duped and I remember their laughter, full and easy and derisive as they sat in the shadows. Building my first house was like reaching for that wallet. The files were meant to convince me that I was organized, that I knew what the hell I was doing. I knew diddly-squat.

Each file houses lined paper with that day's to-do list, sometimes twenty items long. There are also lengthy lists of questions, phone numbers everywhere, photocopied articles from building magazines, thick brochures from window manufacturers, old blueprints, my poor drawings, and numbers, numbers, numbers. I loathe numbers, love words. And like the bones song ("the hip bone's connected to the, thigh bone, the thigh bone's connected to the, ..."), the files are often interrelated, each decision impinging on a dozen others. Some stray pieces of paper *do* amuse, like the one in the Plans file showing Kurt's drawing of his proposed kitchen layout for the cabin. Like medieval or folk art, the rendition was one-dimensional, which gave it charm.

Any first-time contractor would have faced similar challenges to mine, but nothing about the old log cabin was standard or conventional. Every tradesman had to pause, scratch his head about this or that, spend a little, or a lot, more time. And time, I would learn, was money. Time was also the enemy.

Charles McRaven, who wrote *Building and Restoring the Hewn Log House,* one of the bibles of log house redemption, observes that "the square-logged homesteaders' house of this country's uplands is an architectural form entirely its own ... And the labour involved was staggering. If there is a single reason hewn log houses are so rarely built today, it is that just too much work is required. Everyone who attempts a log house today tries to avoid the very investment in painstaking, hard work that gave the hewn log house its heart."

A part of me, a soft romantic underlay, sought to pay homage to our rapidly vanishing heritage. Another part of me wanted it done right, with no stinting on materials, and the more money I threw at the place, the fussier I got, the harder I worked.

I remember all too well brushing several coats of black goop onto the foundation walls, an apparently easy job made brutal by horrid heat and humidity, and the awful confines of the tiny space between the eight-foot-high concrete blocks and the earthen wall all around. Only my thinness let me sidle along the length of that space; turning was impossible, reaching low all but impossible. I feared being crushed by falling earth. I hated the thick black gloves and plastic goggles I had to wear as protection against the nasty waterproofing tar. I hated its smell. And I loathed going down into what I called "the airless pit," the wall of county earth behind me, the foundation in my face.

I remember the three of us—my carpenter Michael, my friend David, and I—setting into place atop the foundation the beam that would run the cabin's length. A coalition of two-by-eight white pine three pieces thick and made to stretch some thirty feet long, it was by far the heaviest lumber I had ever shouldered. We gasped at the weight and bulk of it, how it dug into the bones of our shoulders and resisted us.

I remember hauling endless wheelbarrow loads of gravel to the four corners of that vast hole in the ground, then raking it all flat, for this was the bed on which the concrete floor of the basement would eventually sit. Down there you wanted lots of rock to help with drainage. Later, up above, when the grader had finished his work, we would pluck rocks from the earth to make for smoother footing and greener grass. More wheelbarrow loads of rock. I conscripted Kurt and Ulrike and Oma (my wife's mother) into this labour of down-on-hands-and-knees rock picking. There was no end of work and never enough workers.

The old tongue-and-groove pine floorboards were desperate for brush and soap and water. Board and batten wanted bleaching oil. Scaffolding had to be set up, moved, dismantled, trucked back to the rental place in town. Great piles of sawcuts warranted a new home at the kindling pile and away from the work site, which needed cleaning at the end of every workday. In all these endeavours, I was the grunt. When I wasn't helping Michael and the other skilled builders—framing, roofing, installing windows and doors—I had my own raw labour to attend to.

But my sweat equity, and that of family and friends, would pay handsome dividends. House and builder and landscape would meld, and despite the dark and comic twists, the great swath that raising those heritage beams cut through my life and bank account, I would do it again. For in the end (though there is no end, for the cabin remains a work in progress), the rescued cabin rescues me. What took me by surprise was the sense of well-being the cabin would bestow and continues to foster.

When the trees are in foliage, the only other habitation I can see is Jen's white farmhouse and her tall grey barn and outbuildings about half a mile away. I have sat for hours in an Adirondack chair on the lawn facing a point a hundred yards or so to the southeast where three close-knit maples of varying age (I call them The Three Sisters) give me immense pleasure for reasons I do not quite fathom.

One day in June I was sitting in that same chair, facing south and east, when something came over me: a feeling of almost hormonal happiness, powerful and unprecedented, almost electric. The bliss was short-lived; I have not felt it since and am glad, for it was too pure to be trusted. I was smoking my pipe in the shade of the young linden, looking out over the barely stirring field of wheat.

Ulrike was inside, measuring material for the skirt around my island kitchen cupboard—my crude spruce and plywood carpentry at odds with her precision. It irks her that while the lay of the material told her my varnished countertop was high at one end, the level said otherwise. My carpentry reminds me of Grandpa's line about his handiwork. I think he was talking about building the pumphouse at the farm: "I can build all right, but there's no guarantee [in his Irish dialect, *guar* rhymed with *far*] that what I build will stand for long."

The stillness and quiet were cradling me that day. Just singular sounds, the odd fly or bee, one red-winged blackbird who favours the white cedar at the southern edge of the windbreak, that V-shaped line of cedars and spruce that points northwest. Even the near constant county wind seemed to have paused. I imagined that in the fields all around me predator and prey had signed a momentary truce, that mantises left crickets in peace, foxes idly watched voles, hawks dozed in white pines, and birds all dropped their vigilance. I kept staring at that trio of maples to the southeast, as if seeing them for the first time.

We had just that morning encountered a friend after not seeing him for a long time, his marriage shattered, his business "in the toilet" as he put it. And the same thought came to me as has come to me in recent days. I am a lucky man.

I think, I could sit here for an eternity, like a monk. Let that be my monument, let them pour amber over me. Let the sign say, Here Sat a Happy Man. Happy, at least, sitting in that chair while the red-winged blackbird sang his song.

A walk on the land is sometimes its own reward. One mid-December day I was gathering white pine boughs for a wreath, clipping trees we had planted at the edge of the forest in the north field almost ten years before. Nudged only a little by human help, the forest is slowly marching south, with young dogwood and ash and sumac reclaiming this lower section of the field that Farmer Guernsey—who works our land—finds too wet in spring for ploughing and planting. That day, my aforementioned pal David Carpenter and I had each cut a Christmas tree, and it gave us great pleasure knowing that the tree had been planted as a seedling—maybe by Kurt or one of his friends hired on for the day, by Ulrike or Oma, by David or me. David is a close friend, and I am happy to report as I write this that he and his wife, Claudine, own the land across the road, a fact that adds mightily to the cabin's appeal.

That day, it was Dusty who came upon the head of the deer: the eight-point rack still proud against the snow, the kill fairly recent. Though the skull was picked clean, likely by mice, there remained a bracelet of bloodied fur where bone and antler met. We paused to ponder the deer's fate. Shot by a hunter and wounded, then taken by coyotes? A hunter would not have left behind a trophy like this. Maybe old age or disease overtook the deer, maybe his end was noble: did he turn to face the coyotes in order to give the others a chance to flee? I only know that his crown lent a little majesty to the north field that day.

I left the skull but later retrieved it. I have no desire to display the antlers as hunters do; my thought was to give the rack a place of honour and somehow incorporate it into the fabric of the place. The skull I severed and buried; the antlers sat in the shed awaiting some higher purpose.

The day of their discovery, David and I walked south across the sloping north field, by far the biggest of the three fields on the property, and one in which I had initially chosen to situate the cabin. We said little, as close friends of long standing—in our case, thirty-five years—are wont to do.

"What a great field," I said suddenly, and David agreed that it was. The small simple pleasure of walking your own land (though I take as much pleasure walking David's land as I do mine) is one we both well know. That day we were like two Duddy Kravitzes (you will remember that line from the Mordecai Richler novel, "A man without land is nothing"). How often have we congratulated ourselves on sinking what cash we possessed in 1988 as down payment on what we would each call "the land"? Many of our friends, those who could manage it, anyway, had bought cramped cottages on loud lakes. I, too, had once gone that route.

Not shrewd in business, I bought the family cottage in southern Ontario twenty-five years ago because I could not bear to see it go to strangers. The real estate sign on the place, voyeurs tramping around while an agent warbled about the view, me eyeing them with thinly veiled hostility: it was all so much trespass. So, and this made no sense, I bought the place in 1978 while living in British Columbia. Then, and this is the measure of my financial acumen, I sold it in the mid-1980s when circumstances forced my hand and when the cottage market, coincidentally, was at a low ebb. A year after the sale, our old cottage—"Buckhorn," we called it, after the lake it overlooked—was worth more than double my selling price.

I did love that place in the Kawartha Lakes (the Ojibway word *kawatha* means "bright waters and happy land"), about 90 miles northeast of Toronto, and I used to go there with Flip—the shepherd-collie cross whose appetite for letter carriers would one day signal her demise. My parents bought the place in 1963, when I was fourteen. But in time the cottages all around us would become gentrified, and the sounds of aggrandizement and renovation and winterizing—radial saws, hammers, insulation trucks—filled our days. Neighbours kept felling trees to make their lawns ever grander so that the lawn mowers would have more work. What is it about men and machines?

I would load Flip into the aluminum boat with the old five-and-a-half horsepower Evinrude and scoot over to what my siblings called "Larry's Island." The island was just around the point, too small to warrant someone owning it or building on it.

The island's smooth and massive egg-shaped perch of granite offered natural creases, as comfy as any chair, where a young man could read his *Globe* and novel, and the rockface dipped sharply down at water's edge, inviting to both man and dog. We dived in when the sun got too strong, sure of the dark water's depth. Sometimes we'd be there the better part of a day, me hoping the builders back at Buckhorn would go. I longed for cool fall days when I had the place to myself. The value of Buckhorn diminished in my eyes even as its value on paper would later accrue.

My father had routered out the lettering for a wooden sign that he hung by the cottage's red front door: "Larry's Hideaway" (also the name of a then prominent Toronto bar). Alas, the place was becoming less and less a hideaway. Years after I sold it, several of my siblings and I returned, curious about its fate. We hardly recognized the cottage, and while I liked its prouder bearings and bolder outlook, I could not forgive the new owners for cutting down all those trees. In my log cabin today hangs an oil painting of the original Buckhorn, done by a family friend and bequeathed to me in my mother's will. Dad's old hideaway sign hangs on the wall opposite. The old place lives on, and not just in my imagination.

In the county where the cabin sits, there is talk of land soaring in value because vintners have discovered it. The next Okanagan Valley, the next Niagara Escarpment. Some county eyes have been lighting up at the thought. David Hutchison (Hutch), a teaching colleague of David Carpenter's, had enjoined half a dozen of us in the mid-1990s to help him plant hundreds of grape vines on David's land. Hutch is an obsessive and we spent several autumns with our hands in the cold mud, sank posts to graveyard depth, anchored heavy wire with buried concrete blocks to support the vines. We watched in dismay the die-off every spring, watched in summer as birds feasted on our few grapes. Hutch's promise of wine in our dotage was literally withering on those vines.

But Hutch, true to form, kept insanely detailed records, saw what varieties flourished and which failed, dutifully replanted, set up net defences against marauding birds, and all summer long tended the vines as if they were African violets. Years on, Hutch could claim some foresight. It looked like there *would* be wine in our dotage, though I worried that just as good a bet is that we'd find Hutch one day slumped over a vine, clipboard on the ground, a great clutch of grapes in his cold blue hand. "Here Lies Dave Hutchison. Worked Himself to Death," the marker on his grave would say, and an old image would come back to me: Hutch in shorts and gumboots, soiled T-shirt and ball cap, in the dying light of the day (flashlight as likely), following in the path of the pitching and diving rototiller, eyes straight ahead, a smile on his lips. The master vintner dreaming of wine.

It would, we knew, be good wine. One year, Hutch orchestrated a dinner in the county and served up various wines he had made from grapes grown at home in Toronto. He lectures on wine and wins wine-tasting contests. The man knows his grapes, and no one was surprised that his homemade hootch was first-class. Hutch, we would say at his wake, was a wine pioneer.

What we did not know then was that wine and the pioneers were old pals. The Irish, I would learn, had settled this part of Prince Edward County in the early 1800s, and they made a custom of gathering wild grapes and making wine. I found mention of this in a book called *County Yarns,* penned by a doctor who lived in the grand country house I can see when I look south down the field through the hedgerow. Six generations of his family lived in that house; indeed, our road is named after his great-grandfather, who came here from Belfast in 1815. The doctor was much loved ("worshipped," say my neighbours Dick and Anne who now live in his house).

"The wild grapes," wrote the doctor, who was born in 1890, "grew along the fences—the fences were just covered with them, and they would take a day off, several neighbours, and pick these wild grapes and make a very delicious wine. You'd bottle it and put it in the cellar. Seldom drank it unless there were some callers." I'm guessing that the wine was sweet (like the carrot wine an aged neighbour in the country once served me), for this wine was customarily served with cookies. On the other hand, Al Purdy—the rascal poet who built an A-frame at Roblin Lake near the spot where he's buried on the west side of the county—apparently also made wild grape wine that wasn't at all sweet. Today, wild grape still grows in profusion on fencelines and in hedgerows, as thick as strangler figs.

David's brother, Peter, an eccentric with a Santa Claus beard, joined us in those early grape-planting work weekends. Somewhat prematurely, he had "Wicked Point Winery" etched professionally onto the front doors of his white truck. Locals were puzzled. They knew about Wicked Point and its reputation for downing ships in the nineteenth century, but the winery was news to them. There was, and is, no Wicked Point Winery, but six years later, the county boasts forty growers of grapes and a newly formed association of wine growers. Developers are extolling the virtues of the limestone soils in the county and the moderating effect of the lake; they predict that Chardonnay, Riesling, Pinot

Gris, and Pinot Noir will become the focus of a burgeoning wine industry and that by 2005 eight wineries will be selling regional vintages.

David's land, my land, could one day fetch a handsome price. This is not something I long for—and not just because rising land values hike taxes with them, drive out the born-and-breds and change the character of the place. The land will never sell while I breathe (I would rather take work as a telemarketer than sell), and my intention is that the land be set aside as a nature conservancy or as part of a land stewardship program. The cabin and the parcel of land that surrounds it will never be featured in some real estate guide, and that makes it the purchase of a lifetime.

The cabin, and cabins like it all over this continent, is not for everyone. In 1998, the American writer Charles Siebert wrote a book called *Wickerby,* about five months he spent in a ramshackle log cabin "in the Canadian woods" north of Vermont and much removed from his usual digs in Brooklyn. The cabin was near Lake Memphremagog, where the family of the late Mordecai Richler continues to have a summer place. Siebert would sleep at the cabin with an axe in his hand, awake for hours and tensed for the first noise he could not decipher. He longed for the familiar sounds of night and home: gunshots, sirens, "ten-melody car alarms, and riled, drunken conversations from the stoops of the three-story walkups ..." Home, where he slept like a baby.

Siebert saw nature's menace; I see its embrace. The quiet rattled him, soothes me. His time alone at the cabin made him understand why "hermits are always shown in movies wielding shotguns at the approach of strangers." Solitude, or at least a goodly dose of it, seems to make me a better, not a worse, companion. Or such is my claim to Ulrike when I heed the cabin's call.

If pressed, I might cite the inspiration of an eighty-three-year-old woman who had kayaked alone some eight thousand miles along the British Columbia coast, most of it after she had turned sixty. Why *alone*? interviewer Bill Richardson asked her on CBC Radio. Audrey Sutherland replied that the company of others "diluted" her focus from the curious otters and whales that came in close to check out her and her yellow kayak. The woman had worked all her life, been a wife and mother of four. Alone on that coast, feasting on mussels cooked on the shore in the garlic and butter and wine she had brought with her, she was just another creature on the planet. I was struck by the intimacy of the scene she drew, and the ease of her solitude.

David once shocked me by admitting to feeling at times uneasy—Charles Siebert uneasy—in his little bit of booniedom, for what if a loony menaced him and Claudine? We were sitting on the porch of a friend's cabin in the woods, on the Burnt River in the Haliburton Hills. David allowed as how he might one day get a gun and keep it at his trailer. At this, I literally fell off the low porch laughing at the scenario I instantly concocted: David and Claudine huddled in their little house on the prairie while hooligans circled them on horses and fired their guns in the air. "Hey, Claw-deen," David shouts over the gunfire, "I think I winged one." Can't say I shamed him, but there has been no further mention of sidearms.

In a way, Charles Siebert actually likes the cabin, but he would prefer it to exist on top of, say, a high-rise, as one rich and eccentric Manhattanite put his. The Quebec woods and its creatures were too foreign a canvas for too urban an artist. Siebert had assured his reader that he "hadn't left Brooklyn to achieve some Thoreauvian ideal, to shed all inventions and conventions by way of arriving at a more essential self." He was no "modern man playing at primitivism." And I thought, what's wrong with play? What's wrong with primitivism?

("Modern man playing at primitivism" has long fascinated us. On August 19, 1913, an illustrator named Joseph Knowles announced with great fanfare—he was naked as he headed into the Maine woods and waved goodbye to reporters—that he aimed to live "as Adam lived" for sixty days. In his regular dispatches to the *Boston Post,* written with charcoal on birchbark, Knowles said he rubbed sticks to make fire, wove strips of bark to produce clothing, and hunted and fished. He emerged from the bush two months later clad in bearskin and looking ragged but apparently in good health. Newspapers across the country had followed his adventures, cheering crowds gave him a hero's welcome and snapped up his book *Alone in the Wilderness,* which sold a staggering three hundred thousand copies. And when a rival newspaper to the *Post* published evidence that Knowles was a fraud whose "Nature Man" adventure had taken place in a cabin in the woods, there were denials all around. A lot of people wanted to believe the story and could not face the fact that they'd been duped.)

Yet Siebert's point about "playing at primitivism" must resonate. Lots of people have come to our cabin and I marvel that they do not marvel. They see the rustic enterprise as quaint and backward, perversely so. Other visitors run their hands over the wide timbers; they lounge in the privacy of the place, the sense of space both outside and in, how you can stand in the middle of the cabin at the heavy vertical supporting beam and look out two large windows in each of three directions—north, south and west—and out tall French doors on the east. The open concept, the ten-foot ceilings, the enlarged windows and absence of any curtains, the cabin's location in mid-field, all ensure that light pours in. I have since added screen doors on the north and south sides (with glass inserts for winter); for me there can never be enough light. I love the embrace of the surrounding fields and have begun to carve out breaks in the hedgerows so that our own fields to the north and south, and fields beyond them, and the forests farther on all become part of the cabin's purview.

One couple, old friends closing in on retirement from teaching, were so keen on the feel of the place that they cast their net in county waters: they called a real estate agent. They wanted what we had: a little land, a little cabin, a little peace.

Another couple, Bob Gregoire and Marilyn Smith, raised on the prairie, arrived late one summer evening for their first glimpse of the place and it was an hour before they came in, so intent were they on admiring, and photographing, the cabin silhouetted against the moon and the night sky. I supped on their glee. In the morning the flat expanse of honeyed wheat—though quaint by prairie dimensions—put them back in rural Manitoba.

A visiting teenager from France had never seen a firefly before, and the sight of thousands of them in a vast field, sparkling like stars a few feet off the ground, put him into a private thrall.

Pierre-Édouard stayed out there for an hour, came into the cabin with a firefly in a jar and a broad smile on his lips, pronounced the whole experience "vachement bien."

At Loghouse Larry's, as neighbour Jen calls the cabin, ritual is everything: the company of Dusty the dog, going down the road to watch the sun set on Lake Ontario, staring into the woodstove fire when the cold calls for it, settling into the hammock to watch the shooting stars, coyotes calling in the night and deer coming in close on misty spring mornings with Miles Davis on the boom box, the coffee on, and the French doors open wide to let in the chatter of birds and the county's notoriously bold breezes.

The phone never rings at the cabin, not even the cellular kind, for neither has a place here (though I can always be reached in a pinch, through neighbours). There will never be a television or VCR at the cabin either, no fax machine, no beeper. Retro man likes his retreat free of distractions. I do play CDs—John Lee Hooker, John Coltrane, Van Morrison, Keith Jarrett, Oscar Peterson. Only in the morning do I let CBC Radio into the sanctuary, and so the morning of September 11, 2001, unfolded for me in the cabin. And, like many people, my instinct was to go to a phone—David and Claudine inherited her mother's place in a village close by and had given me a key. Call home. Connect. That night I walked Dusty along the quiet road that fronts the cabin and there was something in the air. George Bush would have called it the smell of "evildoers."

A friend with asthma tells me that the air in the county where the cabin sits is the best in southern Ontario (which may be damning with faint praise, for southern Ontario air can be vile during summer heat waves). Part of the illusion of the cabin is this notion that the air is somehow better there, and most times of the year it is. But this night there came on the south wind a whiff of something sour and metallic. My nose had never known such a thing—not here, not anywhere. For perhaps the only time, I left the cabin the next day without the usual sadness and regret. That morning, I just wanted home. To see Ulrike and Kurt, to count fingers and toes and blessings. On September 12, true home was where I wanted to be. Most times, though, I am glad to go to the cabin and sorry to leave it. In the summer I'll stay for a week at a time, writing in the morning on my old laptop. Amused by the antiquity of my computer, an editor friend in Toronto always asks how my old Gestetner is working. Afternoons at the cabin are reserved for some sort of physical or manual labour—modest carpentry, painting, cutting and splitting wood, maintenance, repair.

In the summer of 2001, I set into the ground five heavy round beams that heretofore had been parked on skids in the high grass north of the cabin, along with some other remnants of the cabin's deconstruction, all waiting for some new duty. In 1827, the beams would have supported the cabin's roof, but I was more inclined to give that job to new and bigger wood; the building inspector thought likewise. Two of the beams would be cut and pressed into vertical service as support for a hammock beneath a young maple; three other beams would form a triangle and receive a privacy siding of barnboard also rescued from the cabin—all part of an outdoor solar shower. This simple rig is one that campers often deploy: the sun heats up the water in a black plastic ten-gallon bag, and a tiny showerhead delivers the water. Here, I thought, here the found antlers would come into play. Only someone using the outdoor shower would see the rack fixed to the six-foot-high barnboard. Naked to the field behind, embraced by the V shape of the barnboard, the Adam or Eve in the shower would hang his or her clothes and towel on a buck's majestic crown.

David and I had used a two-man, gas-powered auger to make the holes for the rig's supporting beams, and sometimes we'd hit rock and the digger's chainsaw engine would toss us around like broncs toss cowboys at the rodeo. We would laugh and go back to work. The manual labour I do at home out of duty I do at the cabin joyfully. Go figure, Ulrike says. Or something like it.

What sets the cabin apart is that it exists as a state of refuge, a little out of time and space. There, I am that boy in his tree fort, and though it is in some ways primitive and roughshod, it is mine. One summer, Kurt and his friend Jack scouted all forty-three acres before choosing the site for their tree fort—where the driveway meets the road. Two summers later, Kurt and another friend from France, Matthieu, added another platform much higher up the tree. And just as Kurt and Jack and Matthieu like the view from their fort, I like the view from the cabin. The world seems a better place there.

The old Toshiba lets me write at the cabin but could no more bring me e-mail than a horse-drawn carriage could fly. As I write this, there are plans to introduce running water to the cabin—some day; and a composting toilet may one day complement my sturdy privy in the hedgerow (and the antique commode I bought for "emergencies," in what I call the bathroom upstairs). An architect friend in Toronto—the aforementioned Bob Gregoire—drew up plans for a proper staircase, with winders, to replace the "temporary" and perilously steep set that my carpenter, Michael, had built in 1997. The new set, a rather glorious configuration of ash and pine and oak, was installed last spring, and I call it l'escalier Gregoire (he was born a Franco-Manitoban) in his honour. An electric stove (I am the benefactor of friends' divorces and remarriages) will soon displace the hot plate; the old cooler with ice packs has already yielded to Oma's fridge. The cabin has long had electricity, but the cable is buried lest overhead wires taint that pioneer look. Friends and family are bemused, say I was born in the wrong century, but none can deny that my time at the cabin helps keeps me grounded and sane.

The cabin is not merely quiet, but *assuredly* quiet, and I can put no value on that. I have been known to pack the old Nissan truck—with water, food, boom box, and dog—at nine of an evening when one neighbour's backyard party or another's near-round-the-clock construction noise was threatening to unhinge me. All my life, noise has been the bane of me. When I was a young man, I once slept at my grandmother's house in Belleville, Ontario, and she was happy to have had me as a guest and insisted that I take her bed and she the couch. But where, she wondered later, did her alarm clock go? I had wrapped the heavy old ticker in a silencing sock and plunked it in a drawer. Ulrike and I moved to a village and lived there for seventeen years in part (my part, anyway) because city noise had murdered sleep, to paraphrase the bard.

Yes, let's talk about noise. *Noise,* from the Latin *noxia,* meaning injury or hurt. In the early 1990s, Chris Czajkowski began writing letters to (the now sadly departed) Peter Gzowski when he was host of CBC Radio's flagship national program, *Morningside.* An independent woman of unusual bent, she was building with little help a log cabin near the aptly named Lonesome Lake in west-central British Columbia, and her letters would form an elegant book, *Cabin at Singing River: Building a Home in the Wilderness.*

Here is Czajkowski, explaining what it's like to re-enter the urban environment after months at her cabin. "I am overwhelmed by the noise. Electric houses hum and furnaces roar. Televisions and radios slam out gossip and jingles in a bewildering manner, and each competes with the other for loudness and sensation. It is sad to think that most people are so numbed by it that they no longer hear it."

In many households, the television is on as "background" noise, with vacuum cleaners, coffee grinders, video games, printers, radios, microwave ovens, blenders, dishwashers, humidifiers, and dehumidifiers fading in and out of an interior soundscape that derives completely from machines. Outside, cars and trucks and planes and lawnmowers (don't get me started on leafblowers, Whipper Snippers, and car alarms), skate boarders, builders and renovators and civic workers (operating garbage and recycling trucks, chipper machines, chainsaws, street sweepers, sewer suckers) ensure that urban quiet is rare at best, and certainly not to be counted on. The assault is near constant, and a growing body of scientific evidence suggests that noise—interior and exterior—is not just irksome and harmful to our hearing but damaging to our health.

Intrusive noise has been linked to higher blood pressure, lower productivity, and higher serum-cholesterol levels.

Psychological studies suggest that continuous noise makes us less caring, less communicative, less reflective, and more inclined to feel helpless and powerless. Noise feeds aggressive behaviour (so far, only in my dreams have I dispatched callously noisy neighbours). Noise contributes to learning problems and leads to fatigue as the body struggles to adjust to the din of modern life.

The Canadian composer R. Murray Schafer has thoughts on all this. In his book *Voices of Tyranny, Temples of Silence,* he argues that noise inhibits awareness at all levels. In *The Tuning of the World,* he introduces the notions of "sound power" and "sound imperialism"—think of how someone with a loudspeaker can control acoustic space. Schafer also reminds us that while the pre-industrial world was quieter than ours, it was not quiet. Julius Caesar virtually passed an anti-noise bylaw in 44 BC. "Henceforth," the emperor proclaimed, "no wheeled vehicles whatsoever will be allowed within the precincts of the city, from sunrise until the hour before dusk ..."

Schafer also champions the merits of listening and of respecting silence. One exercise he often gave to his students was to try a moratorium on speech for an entire day. Just listen. "It is a challenging and even frightening exercise," he wrote in *The Tuning of the World,* "and not everyone can accomplish it, but those who do speak of it afterward as a special event in their lives."

"In the past," wrote Schafer, "there were muted sanctuaries where anyone suffering from sound fatigue could go into retirement for recomposure of the psyche. It might be in the woods, or out at sea, or on a snowy mountainside in winter. One would look up at the stars or the soundless soaring of the birds and be at peace." That's precisely what I do. The cabin is my muted sanctuary.

The word *sanctuary,* meaning sacred place, has lost the power it once held. Christian churches were given the right of sanctuary by Constantine I, and fugitive slaves felt safe there. In ancient Egypt, the temples of Osiris and Amon offered the right of sanctuary, as did the Greek Temple of Apollo at Delphi. The same held true through the Middle Ages, when it was considered sacrilegious to remove a person from sanctuary. Modern penal codes, alas, no longer recognize the concept. In many cases of contemporary tribal and ethnic violence—in Central America, Africa, and the Balkans—whole villages gathered inside a church for safety only to be burned alive, hacked to death with machetes, or sprayed by machine-gun fire.

On the other hand, I have been struck by how many people in my acquaintance have their own safe places. A friend of mine, an avid birder and an emergency room physician, has promised to take me to a 123-acre piece of land he and his family own on the Nova Scotia coast. "There's a cliff," he says, "overlooking the ocean. I go there to meditate." Even people I know who live in the country, on several hundred acres set on lonely roads, have built cabins in the woods.

We find sanctuary where we can. When I lived in Toronto more than a decade ago, I had a stressful job in radio, one I had taken on the advice of a friend and colleague who had done similar work with the same national program (*Morningside,* with Peter Gzowski). "There's a large botanical garden under glass," he told me, "just down the street from the office. There will be days when the job will unravel you. Go there—on your lunch or break. The crystal palace will act like a hot compress on sore muscles." And indeed it did. The Allen Gardens conservatory, built in the

1930s as a kind of jewel in the crown of a once splendid park, was thick with tropical plants, and when you shut its heavy glass doors, you also shut out the noise of the city. I remember feeling embraced by tall lush greenery, the sweet perfume of damp earth, the sound of trickling water. I remember breathing deeply while sitting on one of the several benches placed there. I would return to my work, the pressing deadlines, the ringing phones, the unfinished scripts, refreshed from my time in the rainforest.

Going on a retreat, and even a silent retreat, is an ancient tradition in the Catholic and Buddhist religions. I remember the Irish priests at the Catholic high school in Toronto I attended inflicting on us periods of silent retreat; I wasn't ready for it then. Perhaps I had too much to say. Or was it that walking the football field behind the school failed as meditative setting?

In one of his poems, "Burnt Norton," written in 1935, T.S. Eliot has a line about "the still point of the turning world." But maybe you must be of a certain age, must have sustained a few of life's body blows, before you can appreciate what comes with stillness and silence. In 2002, almost two thousand people went to the Villa Marguerite, a Catholic-run retreat in Quebec, as a way of dealing with the stress of ordinary life. The Montreal chapter of Alcoholics Anonymous holds its annual retreat there. Part of the routine is what one nun calls "integration prayer," a ritual that involves bowing in four directions and invoking the blessings of both the day and the earth. People addicted to alcohol or recovering from heart attacks or cancer or simply under siege from cellphones and deadlines are finding that quiet time in nature allows them to slow down to breathing pace, lets the mind clear, the body pause.

Pierre Levy, a social scientist at the University of Ottawa who has gone on twenty silent retreats in both Canada and Europe, is convinced of their salubrious effects, but that's not why he goes on them. "The silence," he says, "is an oasis in the middle of the desert. It's a rest from constant interaction—you stop running and realize who you are." At the Villa Marguerite, Sister Maureen Wild is convinced that connecting to beauty and nature are central to the healing power of silent retreat. "We go out of our retreat experience," she says, "deepened in our relationship to humans and the whole of creation."

Recently I read an interview in the *Ottawa Citizen* with the novelist and travel writer Pico Iyer. Four times a year he goes to a Benedictine monastery in northern California. "The minute I get out of the car," he says, "my head stops spinning. I forget everything in that protected space and in the absolute silence. When I leave, it lasts for three to five days and then the peace is gone."

My sister Karen, who recently went on a trip to the Serengeti Plain, talks about the cleansing effect of being in the pure silence of the African wilderness for three weeks. During all that time, they never travelled faster than twenty miles an hour in a Land Rover. Her first day back in Toronto, commuting to work on the helter-skelter Highway 401—something she had done for decades—frightened her for the first time. As for the noise, it, too, seemed overwhelming.

For Father Charles Brandt, silent retreat to nature is not an occasional foray, but his life's work. A hermit priest, he lives alone in an isolated cedar house he built himself amid thirty acres of dense forest by the Oyster River on Vancouver Island. I interviewed him in October 1993 when I was a producer with *Morningside,* a preamble to the on-air chat with the program's host. Father Brandt had been profiled on CBC TV's *Man Alive,* as well as in *Harrowsmith* magazine. For a hermit, I told Peter in a background note, he gets around. And I do think his life is bizarre. But I also think he has things to teach us about the need to be alone, the need to reflect, and the need to connect with the earth as our ancestors did.

The hermit priest was seventy years old when we talked to him, and I have never forgotten his sense of humour, his optimism, and the ceaseless challenge of his life's work—to be alone. To walk and meditate, to pray for a sweeter fate for mother earth. Above all, to pay attention, to focus. "We're so cluttered up, so distracted," he told me on the phone (yes, he has one, plus a television and a Volkswagen van) before the on-air interview. "You have to set aside time," he said, "a period of quiet and calm." He admitted to being terrifically lonely at times, but he also cherished what he called "my own little monastery" and found great joy in it. "I never think of leaving here."

Father Brandt rises at 5:00 a.m., the dawn his call to prayer and meditation. His day might be spent tying flies (he is an avid fisherman), preserving and binding books or restoring watercolours (heeding the monk's tradition that each hermit "must earn his own bread"), or preparing the courses he teaches on meditation or on book preservation. Every few weeks he meets with a scientist, a lawyer, a teacher, and a banker to meditate and engage in intellectual and religious discussion. The hermit's answer to poker with the boys.

And if Father Brandt's calling is unusual, so is the journey that brought him to this cabin in the woods. He was born in Kansas City, Missouri, in 1923. His childhood hero was Henry David Thoreau, who went into the woods—as Father Brandt put it—"to see what life was all about." Brandt served as a navigator in the U.S. Air Force and earned degrees in science (his major was ornithology) and divinity. In 1951, he was ordained an Anglican priest but converted to Catholicism five years later and became a Trappist monk, living in a colony with other monks by the Tsolum River on Vancouver Island. Eventually, the colony grew too large and Father Brandt set up his own retreat.

"We are reinventing," he told me, "what it means to be human. Something happened to our humanity. At one point, all men were contemplative. I think it is so important to realize that we are part of the Earth and the Earth is part of us." What he feels on the river is what First Peoples would have felt before the Europeans arrived, this sense that the universe is filled with spirits, including the Great Spirit. That all changed, he says, in the seventeenth century when philosophers and scientists such as Descartes, Galileo, and Newton argued that the universe was mechanically run, without soul or centre. "Now," says Father Brandt, "quantum physicists are telling us that the universe is a complicated web of interdependent relationships."

I took the priest to mean that we should do as he does, or at least as far as we are able. "We must all become monks in a sense," he said. "It's a solitary inward adventure. We are all seeking God in one way or another." For that quest, he said, we need breaks from cities, from materialism, and from the noise that both engender. He was convinced that unless we spend at least some time alone and in nature, we will never understand ourselves or our place in the cosmos.

You can be blind to the truth, deaf to it as well. Some ten million people in the United States suffer from noise-induced hearing loss, says that country's National Institutes of Health. Some twenty million Americans are exposed daily to noise levels that will permanently damage their hearing. Think of rock musicians and their speakers, firefighters and sirens, machinists and drill presses, servers in bars who must endure the nightly din. In New York City, the Noise Center—operated by the League for the Hard of Hearing—has been offering free testing for many thousands of New Yorkers since 1980. In 1991, 28 per cent failed the test (that is, they could not hear various pitches at twenty decibels). In 1998, the figure was 42 per cent, and in 2000 it was 60 per cent. The director of the Noise Center, Nancy B. Nadler, told the *New York Times* that the results are "really shocking. It's frightening, actually."

A word on decibels, a unit of measurement that derives from the name of Alexander Graham Bell. One decibel is a fraction above the lowest sound a human can hear. A person quietly breathing makes 10 decibels of noise. In a forest where only the odd bird or animal makes a sound, ambient levels may reach 30 decibels. Office noise may hit 60 decibels or more, and some alarm clocks reach 80. Rush-hour traffic will easily exceed 90 decibels. Bars and cinemas often achieve noise levels just under 100 decibels, and rock concerts routinely produce sound above 100 decibels. A thunderclap, a plane taking off, blasting disco music—all are in the 120-decibel range, and prolonged exposure at that level does permanent damage to hearing. A child's toy xylophone was found to make 129 decibels of noise. Some car stereos are capable of hitting volumes as high as 150 decibels, while handguns and fireworks make sounds as loud as 170 and 190 decibels.

In her book *Noise: The New Menace,* science writer Lucy Kavaler notes that "when sound levels pass 70 decibels, blood vessels in the extremities constrict, making fingers and toes feel cold, while at the same time blood flow to the brain increases. The adrenal and pituitary glands, which govern a host of body functions, are stimulated and adrenal epinephrine, ACTH, and other hormones come rushing into the bloodstream ..." The mouth goes dry, the stomach churns. The main physiological response to noise, says Kavaler, is fear. And long after the noise has stopped, the changes induced by noise are still fading.

Deep inside the human ear are tiny hair cells that help transmit sound to the brain. Loud sounds damage those cells. Audiologists liken it to the effect of walking on grass repeatedly. At first, the blades of grass spring back, but over time they cease to rebound, the grass turns yellow and dies.

In this country, the Hearing Foundation of Canada reports that Canadians are losing their hearing faster than any previous generation. "We are seeing an increase in people in their forties and fifties with hearing problems," says Dr. David Goldfarb of North York General Hospital in Toronto. "They are the first generation," he told the *Globe and Mail,* "to be born and raised on rock music, gas-powered lawn mowers, traffic gridlock and other everyday threats to our hearing."

One recent fall day, Karen Vye, a specialist on noise-induced hearing loss with Ontario's Workplace Safety and Insurance Board, took ambient noise level readings at various places in downtown Toronto. A friend of hers, the writer Joe Fiorito, was gathering material for a newspaper column. According to guidelines proposed by the Toronto Board of Health, ambient readings should be in the range of 55 decibels. Here is what she found. In the subway, St. Andrew station to be precise, Vye measured 80 decibels, with a spike of 100 decibels when the train entered the station. Front Street—and this was not during rush hour—issued 74 decibels, and the underground food court at First Canadian Place during lunch hour peaked at 82 decibels. At such levels, one must shout to be heard, and the rule of thumb among Vye and other hearing-loss experts is that having to shout to be heard means some level of hearing loss.

Until fairly recently in human history, the loudest sound produced by humans was the ring of a blacksmith's hammer or the din of war. The first mention of industrial deafness occurs in a book called *De Morbis Artificium (Diseases of Workers)* in 1713—making noise-induced deafness a rather recent phenomenon. Vye told me that noise-induced hearing loss dates from the Industrial Revolution. "They used to call it the boiler room ear," she said, "when it was found that men who worked next to these roaring machines were going deaf. The problem with noise-induced hearing loss is that it's on the back burner. There's no drama in noise-induced hearing loss, not when it occurs slowly over a twenty-year period. No one dies or bleeds from gradual deafness."

Even over the telephone, I felt a quick kinship with Karen Vye, who had lived in places I once called home and who had her own cabin story to tell. "In 1977, when I was twenty-five years old," she told me, "I worked for two years in the bush around Hearst and Hornepayne, in northern Ontario [just down the rail line from my boyhood town of Nakina]. I was working for the Ministry of Natural Resources as a research technician, taking a fish census. It was one of the best experiences of my life. Changed my whole perspective." Vye had originally gone into the bush to live in a small cabin with another woman, also a researcher. The place had a small fridge and stove, plus outdoor privy. But the solitude deeply unsettled her co-worker and, within three months and for the next two years, it was pretty much just Vye, her dog, and the wild. She missed hot baths, but the northern lights more than compensated.

"There was a sense of peace up there," Vye recalled. "My job now is to make the world a quieter place, and it's all because of that experience. It's why I'm so passionate about it." Today she lives on a virtual island (accessible by causeway) on Lake Scugog, northeast of Toronto. Before that Vye lived for ten years in Scarborough, where I had lived in my youth and where there was, Vye said, constant ambient noise—"even in my bathtub." It was only when she moved to the quiet of the island that she began to hear, and be annoyed by, the ticking of a wall clock she had owned all that time.

It isn't just urban noise itself that causes stress, but what goes with the territory. "Joe Fiorito," says Vye, "tells me that sometimes there'll be kids skateboarding outside his house when he's trying to write. His blood pressure goes up, first from the noise, and then because he has to decide whether to confront those kids or let it pass. When I convince workers to wear ear protection on the job, the first thing they notice is that they feel less fatigue. Their stress levels go down. Our generation is the first to have to deal with this level of noise. We're guinea pigs." And Vye has no idea how this earsplitting experiment will end.

Even pain, the body's usual response to trauma, fails to alert us to damaging noise. Vye said that at 85 decibels, hearing loss begins; but a 747 revving up doesn't actually cause pain until it hits 125 decibels. Vye is convinced that noise causes stress, which in turn can make people in the city rude and pushy and selfish—especially in traffic. Armed with a sense of humour about some of this, she is convinced that road rage would cease if all the radio stations in Toronto, say, were to play "Smoke Gets in Your Eyes," by The Platters, during rush hours.

A group called the Right to Quiet Society has formed in the face of some worrisome trends. Studies show, for example, that the level of urban din doubles every decade. And since 1973, when the U.S. Department of Housing and Urban Development began to measure neighbourhood dissatisfaction, its leading cause has been—year in, year out—noise. I remember being in New York City at a magazine editors' conference in the early 1990s, and how stepping outside my hotel in the morning was to be greeted with a great wall of manufactured sound. Horns, motors, pneumatic drills. The modern city has a heavy tread, and few heavier than Manhattan's. In 1996, when New York City set up a hotline to help curb minor crime, switchboard operators reported one overriding complaint: noise.

Sometimes the noise is too much, and people snap. People like Lambrinos Lykouresis, a seventy-eight-year-old retired farmer on the Greek island of Zakynthos. He had complained to his neighbour about loud music for months, and one evening, May 31, 1996, Lykouresis could take no more. The old man took his hunting rifle and shot both the woman next door and her twenty-four-year-old son, and now languishes in prison.

Curiously, and thankfully, the Greek farmer marks an exception: as a rule, we seem resigned to noise pollution. Curbing it is complicated and often impossible; easier to mask it. At a hotel in Pegnitz, Germany, for example, guests can escape the noise of traffic by retreating to gardens behind the hotel featuring a computer-controlled soundscape. Directional microphones track the noise of approaching vehicles and relay that information to a computer, which then adjusts the volume of classical speakers in the garden. Light traffic might mean that guests hear Mozart; for rush hour traffic it's Wagner's *Das Rheingold.*

In Paris, meanwhile, technicians were called in to address the problem of high-speed trains barrelling through the station at Roissy Airport. The 112-mile-an-hour train generates noise exceeding 100 decibels, capable of harming hearing. Computers again to the rescue. When the train approaches within half a mile of Roissy, speakers are programmed to play rhythmic, synthesized music that plays loudest as the train pulls in and then diminishes as the train departs. The thinking is that the ear, by being gradually prepared for the sonic blow, is less likely to be traumatized by it.

Travellers sometimes carry with them portable "sound therapy" machines—I see them being pitched in *National Geographic* catalogues, the *Globe and Mail*'s travel section, airline in-flight magazines—to enable sleep and to counter noise from hotel elevators, ice and vending machines, other guests, or city traffic. Such machines are meant to imitate natural sounds—a chorus of insects in a tropical forest, the rhythms of ocean surf, the babble of brooks. One machine, called the Travel Sound Soother, offers twenty sound options—most of them from nature (though two of them, in deference to Charles Siebert and his ilk, issue city traffic and train sounds).

In the fall of 2003, Montreal embarked on its own three-week-long sound therapy experiment. Residents in that city's Notre-Dame-de-Grâce district seem stoic and do not complain about traffic noise from the nearby Décarie Expressway, a sunken, six-lane highway that sees one hundred and eighty thousand vehicles every twenty-four hours. It was the sudden and unpredictable noise of nighttime construction—jackhammers, high-pitched water hoses, and beeping dump trucks—that woke everyone up. One woman called Quebec's Transport Ministry to say that she was at the end of her rope and "had lost her will to live." The ministry decided to rent rock-concert-size loudspeakers, put them in the beds of pickup trucks, and broadcast the sound of surf crashing on a shore. One resident joked that he had to get up to use the washroom more often, but a McGill University history student says she's sleeping better and more easily. "It sounds," says Erin Corber, "like it's raining all the time."

In summer 2002, I happened to be reading the *Atlantic Monthly* when I spotted a full-page ad for a Bose headset. "Use it as a concert hall—or a sanctuary," the words implored. The word *sanctuary* drew my eyes, but the sanctuary they had in mind was not one you go to, but one you carve out for yourself wherever you are. The headphones were being pitched as "a Mute button" for a world of noise—from airplane engines, traffic, offices, and neighborhoods. The headset wearer would hear music or that ever-elusive sound—silence. The stated promise was of a little peace, of blessed quiet, as if the headset itself were on the side of quiet. In a perfect brought-to-you-by-Bose world, I suppose we'd all wear these headsets—much as the Japanese wear surgical masks against polluted air. Only later did I spot one of the tiny accompanying photographs showing a man deploying a leaf-blower while using his "QuietComfort Acoustic Noise Cancelling Headset." A man, in other words, having his cake and eating it.

The technology that permits "noise cancelling" has been deployed in another device called "the Silence Machine." Developed by an engineer at the University of Huddersfield in Yorkshire, England, it works by analyzing the stream of sound waves from a noise source—a pneumatic drill, say, or the bass beat from a nightclub—and then generating sound that is precisely out of phase with it. The resulting "personal sound shadow" ostensibly screens out the offensive stuff and lets in everything else.

The Silence Machine won't be cheap. Industrial models might go for ten thousand pounds (about twenty-four thousand Canadian dollars); domestic versions might retail for a thousand pounds. It all comes too late for Lambrinos Lykouresis, who couldn't have afforded it anyway.

Marcel Proust wrote his vast and introspective novels in a sound-proof, cork-lined room to shut out the noise of the world. George Bernard Shaw wrote in what he called "the Shelter"—an astonishing eight-foot-square shed. It was austere—plank desk, electric lamp, wicker chair, bookcase, wastepaper basket, a Remington portable typewriter, and a telephone rigged to prohibit incoming calls. The whole thing was set on a central steel pipe (Shaw's idea) so it could be rotated, allowing maximum light from its few windows. The Shelter never was rotated, likely because it got too heavy with books and furniture.

Samuel Clemens (better known as Mark Twain) wrote *The Adventures of Tom Sawyer* and *Huckleberry Finn* in a freestanding octagonal study on a hilltop, a gazebo with windows on all sides. Some mornings, E.B. White, the author of *Charlotte's Web* and a longtime *New Yorker* essayist, wrote in a boathouse by his place on the Maine coast. It was the same size as Thoreau's cabin (ten feet by fifteen feet) and was furnished with only a chair, a bench, a table, an old wooden barrel for a wastebasket, and a woodstove to stave off the cool in spring and fall. A large window hinged at the top could be opened wide to afford a view of the water, though White would have had to turn to his right to see the water. "With only a mouse and a squirrel for company," wrote Scott Elledge, his biographer, "White found that the sparsely furnished boathouse sheltered him better than the large house where his bed was. Here he was a wilder and healthier man."

Eugene O'Neill wrote his early plays in an oceanfront cabin on Cape Cod. Arthur Miller wrote *Death of a Salesman* in a one-room cabin he built in 1949 near his home in Connecticut. Charles Lindbergh, who in 1927 made the first solo nonstop transatlantic flight, wrote about the experience in one of several cabins he built for himself and his wife, the writer Anne Morrow Lindbergh. His book *The Spirit of St. Louis* (also the name of his plane), won the Pulitzer Prize in 1954. Today, his granddaughter, Kristina

Lindbergh, also a writer, runs a company called Tiny House Inc. that builds cabins and restores small structures in Westchester County, New York. "It's heavenly to go up to the cabin to write," she says. "Whenever I go up there, I feel like I'm in a different world."

Here's my question. Why do we think that writers alone need quiet for creativity? The nineteenth-century German philosopher Arthur Schopenhauer once observed that "noise is the most impertinent of all forms of interruption. It is not only an interruption, but also a disruption of thought."

Alan Lightman, a novelist, essayist, and physicist who teaches at the Massachusetts Institute of Technology, delivered the annual Hart House lecture at the University of Toronto in 2002. In his talk, he lamented two great losses that are the price of a wired world: the loss of privacy and the loss of silence. Of the first, he observed that we are "plugged in and connected to the outer world twenty-four hours a day." Of the second, he noted that "we have grown accustomed to a constant background of machine noise wherever we are: cars, radios, televisions, fax machines, telephones and cell phones—buzzes, hums, beeps, clatters and whines."

Lightman remembers as a boy "wasting" the better part of a day watching tadpoles in the shallows of a pond or water grasses swaying in the wind. "The sunlight and soil that nourish my inner self," he now says, "are solitude and personal reflection. When I listen to my inner self, I hear the breathing of my spirit. Those breaths are so tiny and delicate, I need stillness to hear them. I need aloneness to hear them. I need vast, silent spaces in my mind. Without the breathing and the voice of my inner self, I am a prisoner of the world [the wired world] around me."

For two months every summer, Lightman and his family retreat to an island off the Maine coast. His teenage daughters used to suffer withdrawal symptoms, and the island seemed a prison without their video games, computers, and television. But soon enough, the seashore would beckon. Lightman explained to me in a letter that his daughters are seventeen and twenty-three now and they have grown up spending large parts of their summers on the island. "Their adaptations to island life over the years," he wrote, "have varied with their ages. The younger daughter needs friends with her to be happy, but the older daughter now loves to have the long periods of silence and seclusion in a natural setting. Both daughters have an intense appreciation of nature—the silences, the clear and dark skies, the sounds of the ocean, the sounds of birds—and quiet contemplation that they would not have had otherwise." Rare visitors, on the other hand, go "stir crazy" after a few days without television, e-mail, or telephone. As for Alan Lightman, he adjusts to island life by putting his watch in a drawer and letting the light and the dark tell him when to sleep and when to rise.

All the noise of the wired world may be anesthetizing the brain and dulling the senses. A controversial European study—reported in *Lilipoh* magazine in 1999—claims that twenty years ago, the average German could hear three hundred thousand distinct sounds. Today, the typical adult hears only one hundred and eighty thousand; many children hear only one hundred thousand.

A landmark study done in 1960 of the Mabaan people in a remote part of Sudan suggests that hearing loss with age is *not* inevitable. A New York ear specialist, Dr. Samuel Rosen, visited these people living in an area of Central Africa virtually cut off from the modern world. The only sounds they hear are the sounds of nature and their own music making, which does not include drums. Dr. Rosen was curious to know whether a quiet society retains its hearing better than a noisy one does, and indeed, this appears to be the case. Where Mabaan men in their seventies suffered a hearing loss of fifteen decibels, comparable American men had lost sixty-five decibels. At eighty, these tribesmen had the same quality of hearing as an American aged thirty. Dr. Rosen wondered whether the difference in each society's "acoustic load" explained the difference. But he also speculated that hearing loss in aging Westerners may owe something not just to noise, but to high blood pressure and atherosclerosis of the small vessels leading to the internal ear. (R. Murray Schafer reports more fully on all this in his book *The Tuning of the World.*)

For Dr. Rosen, noise alone fails to explain why Westerners lose both their hearing and their health sooner than the Mabaans do. "The Mabaans," he wrote, "age more slowly than we do. They have no vascular hypertension, coronary artery disease or duodenal ulcer. They have little atherosclerosis, no allergies or bronchial asthma, and have extremely little stress and strain in their lives ... Might not the stress and strain which afflicts modern civilized man somehow affect *all* [my italics] his senses, including hearing?"

In frustration over lost sleep due to city noise, I once bought earplugs, but they only fuelled my resentment and so they sit in a drawer. They were uncomfortable, ineffectual, and unnatural. Perhaps I wouldn't hear the passing student revellers and skateboarders or the midnight roofer (I'm not making this up), but neither would I hear the smoke detector or my dog pleading to be let out. On hot summer nights, with the windows at home open both to welcome breezes and all the unwelcome noise that cities produce, I sometimes plug in an old and heavy Electrohome fan Oma gave us decades ago (they weren't kidding when they called it the Long Life model). The arrangement is a dubious one. Ulrike cannot abide the noise of the fan, so I decamp to the guest room and plug in my poor man's white noise machine.

At the cabin, sometimes, hounds in the distance will bay—but never for long. The bed is right at a west-facing window, which is always open spring through fall to night sounds: crickets and frogs, nighthawks and coyotes, easterly breezes off the lake riffling through the trees and coursing through the cabin. This is my lullaby. In the morning, the birds start their twitter at dawn and I cannot wait to get downstairs, open up the French doors, and let that ornithological wall of sound *in*. As the summer day heats, the cicadas—which the ancient Greeks kept in cages to better hear their singing—launch their volleys of pure sound. Nature can never be too loud, the city never quiet enough.

Not seven minutes' drive from the cabin is a long and craggy point, one that juts out into Lake Ontario, its apex marked by a classic white lighthouse with a red crown. I remember sitting there one day with my sister Theresa, a Vancouverite who is one year younger than I. We were talking about middle age and finding things to laugh at in that slow spiral the body takes, how fat settles at the hips, how there are jiggles now where muscles were. Tess conceded all that, but, she said, age brings one other thing: after years of struggling to know who you are, you at last come to know what you require. You can't always get what you want, Mick Jagger advised, but maybe, just maybe, you get what you need. And what I need and treasure is this old cabin and the rectangle of land it sits on.

The cabin has its genesis in a magazine article.

In the early 1990s, while on staff at *Harrowsmith,* I wrote a long piece about a man I will call Hal. Alas, I cannot reveal his real name, or those of the tradespeople given parts in my tragicomic, cabin fever epic. Their lawyers might query the hard truths I plan to tell.

Hal was impossibly tall and breathtakingly interesting (though former clients called to paint a different picture after my story was published). He designed and built hybrid houses—stone or wood buildings using original materials from the eighteenth or nineteenth centuries. The facades, inside and out, were old, the guts modern. Hal's house had a foot in two centuries: an antique cupboard hid the dishwasher.

He had on his property a kind of heritage storehouse, a barn teeming with antique floorboards and timbers, doors and windows. And high on a hill overlooking his solitary residence in a valley stood the shells of three nineteenth-century log houses. They were grey ghosts without roofs, their great hewn timbers of white pine dovetailed at the corners, all three of them sitting on concrete blocks and waiting for a buyer.

Hal's prices were beyond me but it was already too late. The notion of living in a piece of Canadian history had me hooked on old logs (as I would get hooked, several years later, by Canadian heritage horses).

Eventually I came to a man I'll call Connor, a bearded imp of Irish blood whose pure passion for things old soon entered my bloodstream like a virus. Connor drew stormy weather the way lightning rods draw flashes, but he was a smooth sailor. Later, I would watch him on the building site and listen to him mutter to himself—humm hummmmmp—when faced with some conundrum. He never swore, never lost it; he seemed faintly amused by problems. It was those around him who were driven to distraction. Like the ex-wife who menaced him one night with a kitchen knife, or the chinker he employed who heaped slanderous abuse on Connor every chance he got. On the few occasions we were in his house, the phone rang constantly, and I had to admire his indifference to the call and his focus on us and our cabin dreams—though later I would fume when it was *my* calls he was ignoring. Connor dashed off sketches on scrap paper to explain details of construction, he told jokes about carpenter ants coming upon log houses and licking their chops, but mostly he made the thought of resurrecting an old cabin sound like a *Boy's Own* adventure. This was early days.

From Connor, Ulrike and I bought salvage rights to a thirty-by-twenty-two-foot, storey-and-a-half white pine log house standing outside Westport, where young soft maples swarmed it.

Forebears of a family called Bresee—there are twelve Bresees in the Westport phone book—had built it as a homestead more than 170 years before, and by the time we chanced upon it, one of their heirs had only recently vacated the red-brick farmhouse that was the cabin's successor. For that was the pattern: pioneers first built a log house and if or when finances improved, the family announced its new standing in the community by building a proper brick farmhouse. The log house then fell to the hired hands, and, eventually, to pigs and chickens.

Connor was in the heritage business: he bought old square-timbered houses and cabins and then resold them, along with his services as builder and contractor. Connor had come to the Bresee farm to rebuild a shed on the back of the elegant red-brick house, one with white keystones at the corners and over the windows. It wasn't long before he noticed and came to admire the log house behind its age-old wrap of board and batten. While the first three courses of logs had succumbed to time and rot, Connor owned plenty of like replacements.

"Would you sell that log house?" he asked Anna Bresee one day at her door.

"What log house?" she replied.

"That one," Connor said, pointing to our future cabin.

"Oh, you mean the pig barn," Mrs. Bresee replied, who was only too happy to sell.

Turns out my father had spent summers as a boy with his cousin, Dick Scanlan, who then still lived in the old homestead across the road with his wife, Monica; during his stays, my father had stolen apples from the Bresee orchard; my grandfather, Terry Scanlan, had carved his initials in barn beams at a farm close by.

This log cabin had my name on it all right. (A log *cabin,* strictly speaking, is a smaller creature than a log *house,* and some people contend that a cabin was of round logs and a house of square hewn logs, but I go against the grain of both definitions: I have always called our house a cabin.)

Connor took Ulrike and me through the log house one day, and I remember rays of sunlight pouring through openings where doors and windows once were. I remember climbing a crude ladder into the hayloft, with a foot of hay all about and the faint and not unpleasant smell of farm animals lending authenticity. I was transported to the barn at my grandparents' farm near Tamworth, where my cousins and I would swing from ropes and high beams—in the manner of pirates boarding ships—into a sea of soft hay below. I was, in other words, hooked. And Connor knew it. Sitting in his truck another day in a pouring rain, we dickered over his price. He held firm; we buckled and bought the place—or, at least, the salvage rights.

Years later, I wrote Anna Bresee, who now lives in Ottawa. Her reply—in a teacher's clear and handsome penmanship—read, in part, as follows:

February 15, 2002

Dear Mr. Scanlan:

Or may I be so bold as to say "Larry"? Since I have talked to Monica Scanlan a few times and much of the conversation was about the old log house, your "fit" with the rest of the Scanlan family, your writing in the Citizen *etc., it almost seems as if you were my next door neighbour.*

Re the article in the paper about your experiences in finally arriving at the finished structure: It was fascinating. I've read it so many times and will be reading it again and again. One odd slant to your story—my son, Dwayne, saw the article when it was first published and he showed it to me and said "That looks like—and reads like—our pig pen from the farm." I didn't give much attention to it for some reason but when Monica gave me the paper I realized Dwayne had shown it to me and I had passed it off as an unlikely circumstance.

We have traced the family tree back to when James Atcheson (my great-grandfather) arrived in Canada from Ireland in 1821 and he must have been in Kingston at first—he was married there in 1823 and settled on the Atcheson farm in 1827 so he must have built the log building as their first home. Their first son John was my grandfather (1831–1887). I remember my father saying he was nine years old when the present brick house was built, so I presume the log house was moved at that time to the barnyard where [Connor] dismantled it.

In the log house, there used to be a large cooker, an iron affair with a fire pot on top, where turnips, potatoes, mash etc. were cooked for the pigs (they had to have their "veggies" too). There were three small doors for the pigs to exit to their separate outside pens. This separation must have been according to the litter age.

At one time, the upper area was used as a chicken "residence." They must have needed that space badly as it seems an awkward place for fowl. Maybe wild animals were threatening the regular coops.

Sorry I can't offer more information. So much past history has escaped because I didn't ask enough questions or listen enough and the old folks are gone now—except me.

In the summer of 2002, I went to see Anna Bresee at her modest little house in the Ottawa suburb of Nepean. She was wearing oversized glasses and her grey hair was cut short; that and her candy-striped dress gave her the look of a youthful volunteer at a hospital. At eighty-four, the former schoolteacher is tiny and bright and full of curiosity. She would hold her gathered fists in her lap and fix her gaze on me, and the more she worried about being of little help to me and my project, the more she talked and the livelier her ancestors became in my mind. Nothing wrong with Anna Bresee's transmitter; it's the receiver that's a little wonky. Anna is hard of hearing and has heard nothing good about hearing aids, so I had to repeat some of my questions twice, but never three times.

Anna Bresee must be made of sturdy stuff. She still drives her own car and was that day intent on cutting her high hedge with electric trimmers, having invited a handyman to bid on the job and having balked at his price. I had hoped that she would one day come to the cabin and see it in the flesh, but the thought of such a long drive—even as a passenger—fatigued her. I would have to content myself with showing her the photo album that chronicled the cabin's slow rise.

"Well," she would say as I flipped each page and detailed the comic and sorrowful details of construction. We sat at her kitchen table and she fussed over the album, as if I were showing off my newborn child.

I wanted to know something of her ancestors, who had built and lived in the cabin. "My great-grandfather, James Atcheson, came from County Tyrone in Ireland," she said. "I am told he was a very strict man. A Methodist. One of his daughters eloped to get away from all that. My grandfather, John Atcheson, was a reeve of Bedford Township, and there is a story that our brick house was built as big as it was because councillors would meet at our house and stay overnight, and the house had to be big enough to accommodate them. Finally, there was my father, Mortimer Atcheson, who was a jolly man in his youth. He was fun. He liked music and used to play the Jew's harp."

Anna Bresee and her sons all live in Ottawa now, but they keep the "Atcheson farm" in Westport and its 177 acres—"more out of nostalgia than anything. It's a place to go." She goes there in good weather and tends a vegetable garden, though the rabbits, deer, skunks, raccoons, and groundhogs often overrun it. Bears now frequent their woods and she is afraid to venture there. But for all her feeling for the place, the old Atcheson farm is also a place tinged with sadness. Three of her father's brothers died tragically in their teens at the property—one drowned in Wolfe Lake, and another was killed after falling off a horse. Anna could not recall the fate of the third brother, and it will likely remain a lost memory, for she is the last surviving Atcheson.

At one point, as we moved through the photo album, she expressed delight at a close-up of one of the beams on the south wall. The photo is of a knot in the wood that either insects of long ago or a playful woodcarver had made into a face, with two wide round holes for eyes and another hole below featuring a protuberance at its centre, like a tongue. Anna got out paper and pen and began to draw the interior layout of "the pig house" as she remembered it, locating the three pigpens and the big stove in the remaining corner where the mash was cooked. I thought of little Anna Atcheson, a child in the 1920s, standing wide-eyed in that barn when it was already a century old and alive with squeals and grunts, clucks and crowing. The place would have been redolent, too, of muck and manure, fresh and rotted straw. In winter, heat from the pigs would have warmed the loft and kept the chickens and their precious eggs from freezing, and maybe that—not fear of predators—explained why it was swine below and fowl above.

Sometimes, after not having been to the cabin for a week or two, and the place having been closed up, I'll open up that north door and be greeted with a smell—of must and dust and old wood. "The cabin smell," Ulrike calls it. Open windows and county breezes soon replace old air with fresh stuff; either that or my nose simply adjusts to what is surely the smell of history.

(As a postscript, you should know that Anna Bresee never realized her hope of seeing her old place. That fall, she suffered two strokes. "She has," her son Dwayne later wrote to me, "diminished mobility and speech capability but I am happy to say she still has a great sense of humour and an active mind." He looked forward to the book, certain that Anna would "recognize the cabin and its tale and be interested in exploring the subject again.")

In 1996, the big pine logs just bought and Connor under contract, the plan was to have his crew dismantle the building, number the logs (a second time, for the Bresees had done the same when they made it a barn), and move them to the secluded parcel of land we own near Lake Ontario, west of Kingston. The cost of establishing what was essentially a summer and weekend retreat had given us years of pause. Finally, my writer's finances as shaky as ever, we dived into the abyss.

What brought the abyss back forcefully was my reading, more recently, of several books. *The Builder's Secret: Learning the Art of Living Through the Craft of Building* gathers tales of amateur builders like me. One man got his house built but lost his wife when the marriage buckled under the multiple strains of construction. Another man remembered assigning an unskilled friend the task of nailing boards in the loft, an experience that left her blistered and exhausted but "all aglow. She talks about it to this day. There is a piece of her in the house. I look at the nails up there, think of her, and smile."

It all seemed achingly familiar. The harmony, the disharmony. *Tower: Faith, Vertigo, and Amateur Construction* spoke to me too. The author, Bill Henderson, hand-built a curious clapboard tower in the woods of Maine—"for no reason," he thought. He came to understand, as I did with my cabin, what intuitive and spiritual sense hard labour makes. It seems that the more we pour ourselves into our shelters, the more we layer in pieces of ourselves.

Ross A. Laird's *Grain of Truth: The Ancient Lessons of Craft* was another book that helped me fathom my physical and spiritual attraction to the cabin. "There is great resonance in things touched and shaped by hands," he wrote, and every time I sit in the rocker in that southwest corner of the cabin and read or smoke my pipe, the timbers tell me that Laird was right. He had argued in his quiet, graceful book that things made by caring hands are somehow *alive,* and maybe that explained why I would sometimes run my hands over the hand-hewn, fourteen-inch-high, eight-inch-thick timbers or gaze up at the massive beams that run the length of the cabin, east to west, and the width, north to south. I remember Connor praising the men who had made the Bresee cabin, for so tightly spaced were the logs that Connor and his men had to use a chainsaw to make space to accommodate the nozzle for injecting the foam insulation that would precede the chinking inside and out.

Our land is more or less flat—its dips and rises are slow and subtle—and quite rectangular in shape. Short sides on the north and south, long sides on the east and west. The approach to the land is from the east: a quiet county road lined with old oaks and maples skirts the property's short southern end and half of its long eastern flank before veering off. The road is neither dirt nor asphalt but something in between, and what I love about our road is how the trees in leaf on either side link overhead to form a canopy. County workers will occasionally park there for lunch on summer days, and I like to think that they are drawn not just to the shade, but to the esthetics of that little stretch. I love to walk that stretch on clear nights, my head cranked skyward to view the stars through the breaks in the canopy. Night or day, the road rewards the walker.

Our three ten-acre fields are divided by, and surrounded by, tall hedgerows, with a thirteen-acre forest at the north end. Three fields and a forest. David and Claudine's thirty-six-acre squared chunk of land across the road is differently arranged: a virtual island of forest surrounded by cultivated fields on all sides but the north one, where the trees kiss the road. The view from the cabin, then, is a pleasing mix of field and forest, of light and dark, of space and tangled growth.

The middle field seemed the obvious choice for the cabin. I remember tromping around in tall clover that spring, testing this or that site, in a loose feng shui way. *Feng shui* means "wind and water" and describes the elaborate ten-century-old Chinese method of determining whether a proposed building site is auspicious, or not. Finally, I marked off a section with stakes and loud yellow trail tape, took my old mower to it, and sat there in the middle on an aluminum lawn chair. A *yep* formed in my head.

It had taken me six years to reach this point. But once we broke ground, the pressure was on. We had to excavate, set the logs on a new foundation, get a roof on, windows in, and chink—all before winter.

"You'll be surprised by how quickly the time goes," warned my lean carpenter, Michael. I had determined that I would set my writing aside for spring, summer, and fall, and work alongside him. Tracy Kidder had written a book called *House,* one that captures the simmering animosities that can fester on a building site among owner, architect, contractor, tradespeople. I thought of that book one day as Michael lectured me—lectured me as an imperious father would a child who had ventured out between parked cars and into traffic—about some small detail of the project and my handling of it. We were parked in my truck outside the building supply store, the one of two in town that Michael had chosen on a hunch (the place would go out of business a year later, the other would survive). The rain was pelting down, hammering on the roof, and the little black Nissan truck I then owned—though blessedly dry—was starting to feel a tad claustrophobic. It wasn't so much what Michael said, it was the tone. Indignation boiled in my head as he droned on. *I'm paying you!* I thought. *How 'bout a little courtesy?*

Michael's fastidiousness—he was more cabinetmaker than carpenter—made him a slow builder, and I was paying him by the hour. But I learned to grit my teeth, hold my tongue, and appreciate his attention to both detail and the bigger picture. There would have been no cabin without Michael.

If anything, the cabin is overbuilt, Michael-built, as are the tool shed and the privy, and though at the time I felt pinched by lumber bills and Michael bills, now I often thank him as I sit on my throne in the hedgerow. I admire the heavy plank door with its Z-shaped inner buttress, the board and batten, the little window on the south wall, the pure heft of it all. In winter, when the privy is nowhere near as welcome a prospect, when the window lets in only a cold light, I think of my mother and her siblings using an outhouse for most of their youth; of course, they fled the farm. Me, I like the privy's utter simplicity, the absence of moving parts and immunity to the vagaries of modern plumbing. And when the privy door is swung open by its occupant, no contemporary *toilette* can boast of such a view.

That spring of 1996, our first order of business was access to the building site. Michael and I lopped off a few cedar posts on the property's eastern flank, peeled back the wire fence, and, with my chainsaw, felled a giant basswood and several small trees to create an entryway, then had a dump truck lay gravel to link county road and site, a hundred yards in. Next we built a shed, a kind of freestanding lean-to. We needed a place out of the rain for us, for tools and lumber. Besides, mice and hornets for miles around had no home and this would be their Hilton. I didn't mind. Building was still new and exhilarating.

We had more gravel trucked in as foundation for the shed, built a rectangular wooden frame overtop, then called in the cement truck to fill its dimensions with soft grey goo. While the pad was still soft, we plopped in anchor bolts—J-bolts, as they are called, with the fish-hook part of the J immersed in the wet cement and only the top showing. Later, when the cement had set flat and hard, we laid down two-by-fours with holes drilled into them to let the threaded bolts poke through, and then tightened down the nuts to marry wood and concrete. Now we had a base, and from it the shed would rise—the first building on the acreage. A photo shows Michael in the doorway of the one wall that was up, the lush green field stretching all around like a yawn in bright sun. His circular saw lies on lumber, the portable generator in the foreground, along with hammers, sawhorses, ladder, two lawn chairs, and plastic tarp. There is an air of busyness, a sense of promise about the work site.

Southwest of the half-built shed, our excavator was making a mess. We wanted a full basement, so Teddy Payne was ripping into the clover, clawing at the land, gouging ever deeper. His backhoe assaulted my ears, and he had an annoying habit of going into facial contortions whenever his machine hit rock and stuttered. He hit rock a lot.

Later, while laying out frames for the foundation, Michael and I discovered that the hole was not dug to specifications: it was too small, too shallow. We called in reinforcements. A menacing machine called a high-hoe would render Teddy's walls properly vertical and hammered away incessantly at the horse-shaped and horse-sized expanse of rock in the centre of the hole. The racket was numbing and the $125-an-hour operator bam-bam-bammed for most of a day. I remember retreating to the privy just to put distance between me and that horrid yellow monster, trying to will it to go. I needed the thing (albeit briefly), but that didn't stop me from hating it.

The issue of who would pay for this added cost, Teddy or me, forced Michael to play peacemaker. Some of my chosen tradespeople would remind me of what a neighbour once said of his grandchildren: "I love to see them come. I love to see them go."

My days fell into a pattern: rise early to drive to the site with Michael, toil alongside him, make runs to the building supply store, then home in the evening to line up the next worker, research the next step in the building process. Every aspect of construction consumed time and money and raised dozens of questions, with each decision impinging on others. For answers I leaned heavily on Michael and on my uncle Rolf, a retired building inspector in northern Ontario. The faxes flew between us.

I learned much. A first-time (and perhaps one-time) contractor, I was the low man on the totem pole of every worker—

mason, chinker, electrician, insulation installer, roofer—whose first allegiance is to known contractors who feed them steady work. Workers, it soon sank in, take on more than they can actually handle since jobs inevitably fall through or are delayed. In this pecking order, a family building a permanent residence would always rank higher than someone like me, the guy building a summer place.

And since the jobs are often linked, each tradesperson has to know my schedule in order to plan his or hers. The dominoes must fall neatly. One worker has the power to hold up or derail the whole job. In the building of my folly, the dominoes did not fall neatly, or easily.

"Where the hell is the mason?" I would ask. "He's good," people would say of the man I'll call Henry, "if you can get him." Well, I couldn't get him. The cement blocks he had ordered sat forlornly in the foundation hole for the better part of the summer. Heavy rain brought mud and minor mudslides. Henry wasn't returning my calls. He had long ago dropped off his mixer and a rusty wheelbarrow.

"It's like a dog peeing on a fire hydrant," I told Michael one morning as we drove to the work site, four weeks from the day Henry was to begin. "He's letting every other mason in the county know that this job is his. Well, I've had it. If he's not here this morning, I'm taking his stuff and putting it at the end of the driveway." I was about to fire my first guy.

But there sat Henry's leaky old pickup in the driveway. Almost the entire east wall of the foundation was in place, so he had to have been there since dawn. The sweat trickled down his face and over his powerful torso, and he looked up at me from the pit.

"Will you ever forgive me, Larry?" he asked.

"I don't know, Henry," I said. "I don't know."

In the cabin's restoration, no one would cause me more anguish. But you had to admire his energy, the way he scurried up the ladder with a heavy ten-inch block on one shoulder. Michael stood in awe of his precision as a bricklayer, and I cherish the fireplace he built, so in the end I guess I did forgive him.

Eventually the cabin could comfortably and happily accommodate the pup and me, and then family and friends. Early each fall—and we have done this ever since the place became suitable for guests—the cabin gathers five male friends I have known for decades, some since the early days of primary school. We barbecue more red meat than we should, drink more beer than is advisable, argue vehemently, and tease relentlessly as old friends will. The cabin is the roundhouse where trains chug in, some early, some on schedule, none late.

Every Thanksgiving, my sprawling Irish-Catholic family (I am the eldest of eight) drives from Toronto and Ottawa; sometimes they fly from beyond—Vancouver, Madrid. One year I flew in myself—from Halifax. We gather at the cabin on Saturday, with up to twenty-six dinner guests arranged around two sets of candle-lit L-shaped tables draped in elegant white cloth. The nephews and nieces sleep in tents in Teddy Payne's basement or in old bunk beds upstairs, and their parents choose either foamies on the floor or local B & Bs. Jen, who operates a catering business in town, delivers the hot turkey dinner, the gravy and dressing and mashed potatoes in sealed containers with snap-down lids, and buns and salads and pies. We play football on the lawn like the Kennedys, sit round a bonfire at night, and we do indeed look up and thank our lucky stars.

One summer, in anticipation of Thanksgiving weekend, I built horseshoe pits alongside the north-south windbreak. A certain brother-in-law almost crowned his own dog with a heavy horseshoe, but as I would later report to a friend, "There were no deaths. No births either. Just a lot of fun." A heavy ping-pong table, bought through the classified ads for seventy-five dollars, was another addition that fall, and the cousins gave it ample use and turned the basement into a kind of rec room when the rains came. That year, we were thankful for *any* rain.

At some point every Thanksgiving, I pile the kids into the truck bed (the count was eleven one year) and head down to the point, and we skip stones on the water at a place Kurt calls Pebble Beach. The kids say that going to Larry's cabin at Thanksgiving is a highlight of their year, better than birthdays. What they crave is its ritual unfolding, and each element must be struck off for the thing to feel complete: the football game leads to the meal, then the long walk in the dark, then the bonfire and the game of hide and seek with flashlights in the dark fields—each little one paired with an older cousin, a safety precaution they devised themselves. I have a vivid memory of two nephews, five and six, whose home addresses, respectively, were then Madrid and Ottawa, each boy armed with a flashlight and a "shield" (pieces of Styrofoam left over from the cabin's construction), walking the tall grass at the edge of the lawn around the cabin. "Let's go exploring," one said to the other. "Yeah," his cousin replied, "we'll look for baby tigers." I was struck by how safe they felt, by their certainty that the only cats out there in the high grass were purring little balls of fur.

Afterwards, the young ones, now spent, sit in the laps of their uncles and aunts and older cousins in the circle round the great crackling bonfire, partake as long as they are able in the banter, and then drift off into the deep and peaceful sleep that comes to a child in the warm embrace of a blood relation, both staring into the flames and embers.

The young ones would leave behind their gifts to the cabin, and the cabin would be glad of them. A homemade candle holder, seeds glued gaily to the side. A drawing of a turkey's head, the wattle a brilliant red, with real black feathers flaring behind. A line drawing of an astonished cow, astonished because she appears to be wearing a saddle pad. Some of this art would be tacked to the cabin's vertical beam, to be remembered next Thanksgiving, when some new wave of homespun crafts would arrive in the clutch of nephews and nieces.

There is something to be said for open spaces, for the way light slants across that field at dusk, for our many and simple rituals, for the square timbers themselves and the stories they have to tell.

fire

The log cabin as we know it is actually an American invention, credited to seventeenth-century Finnish and Swedish colonists on the Delaware River. The square-timbered cabin would work its way north, supplanting other versions of the log house deployed in New France. But, of course, First Nations of the West Coast and the Iroquois around the Great Lakes lived in log dwellings long before the Europeans arrived.

By virtue of its age and key component—wood—the log cabin is a doomed structure. One day my cherished timbers will be firewood. Stone churches endure, but my own small glory, as I call it, is destined for dust. And strangely, I take comfort in that.

One of the great appeals of the land is how life there echoes the great seasonal round of renewal, growth, decline, and dormancy: in spring, I'll coerce family and friends into helping me plant hundreds of seedlings (one year it was twelve hundred). White spruce and Norway spruce, red pine and white pine, sugar maple and red maple, red oak and white oak and bur oak, tamarack and dogwood, white ash and green ash, black walnut, larch, and locust. The six-inch-high locusts we planted in 1989—that first spring when we bought the land—seem to thrive on the rich clay soil and are now more than thirty-five feet tall. Spring 2003 marked the fifteenth straight year we have planted trees. Mortality is high: the plants get too much rain, or too little, they get girdled by mice, nipped by deer and rabbits, choked by grass or weeds, and one year Farmer Guernsey inadvertently beheaded a few hundred seedlings with his harvester. Still, many survive and a young mixed forest has begun to form alongside the tall hedgerow west of the cabin, while the forest to the north—on its own steam and with only a little prodding from us—is expanding ever outward.

In the fall, David and I used to scout our forests for trees to cut—leaners, crowders, the wind-fallen. Our chainsaws in our wheelbarrows, we ranged the now bug-free forest, looking for firewood. One more sustaining ritual. Since I owned the bigger saw, it was my task to fell the tree and then we'd share the work of trimming branches and cutting up limbs and trunks. One autumn in David's forest, we both watched in horror as a chosen tree, a dead maple, all in slow motion turned on its new axis and started to fall—not toward a small clearing as planned, but toward David's outhouse. Fred of Fred's Sheds had delivered the particleboard thing many years before and when the hollow old tree hit, the painted green privy shuddered cartoonishly and bobbed a little, but held.

Maybe one day, Kurt or his children will come to our forest north of the cabin and spend some time under a tree with my name on it. Literally. As much as I love the Point (and I have mused about having my ashes cast on the waters there), I have begun to think that my wrinkled old form—when I'm done with it—might serve a more useful purpose by a certain shagbark hickory or white ash. Maybe the beech grove could use me.

The notion of a "green burial" has gained a certain currency in Britain, where hundreds of woodland and nature reserves have protected status owing to their other use—as burial parks. A like movement is growing in the United States, though the funeral home lobby will doubtless fight it tooth and (coffin) nail. Proponents of green burial find encouragement in the example of the Ramsey Creek Memorial Nature Preserve near Westminster, South Carolina. It's the brainchild of a family doctor and avid conservationist named Billy Campbell, who grew up just miles from the preserve. A photo in *Utne* magazine, where I spotted the story, shows him lying down in a bed of leaves in the forest, hands clasped over his stomach and staring up into the canopy. We test-drive cars; why not burial plots?

"People who buy grave plots at Ramsey Creek," Dr. Campbell was saying in 2002, "are saying no to embalming, to frilly-satin-pillowed, steel-lined, hermetically sealed caskets, to having their bodies turned into Memory Pictures—to all that stuff that so many of us get persuaded to dump thousands of dollars into when death comes knocking on the door." What he proposes emulates what happened in pioneer times: private burials, sometimes on private land. The deceased wrapped in a plain cloth, set in a pine or cedar box, and buried at the foot of a dogwood tree. The county, I know, has its share of family plots in the sacred corners of century farms.

Advocates of green burial point out several drawbacks to the status quo. Cemeteries require almost as much maintenance as golf courses—with much watering needed and heavy use of herbicides. The cost of hardwood casket, funeral arrangements, and headstone can be prohibitive, while cremation consumes energy and contributes to air pollution. Why not simplify everything and boost the cause of nature in one fell swoop? "If just ten per cent of Americans opted for traditional burials in nature preserves," says Dr. Campbell, "land conservation organizations could offer burials that were less expensive overall. Yet collectively they could pull in a billion or more each year in gross revenue." The dream is to restore rundown fields and convert them into healthy forests of native species.

Groups in British Columbia, Florida, California, Washington, Ohio, New York, and Wisconsin are all working on plans to enable what some are calling "green goodbyes." There are no headstones in such parks, only an inscription on a fieldstone marker, or perhaps a plaque on a nearby tree or bench.

In Sweden, meanwhile, a biologist offers this alternative to cremation: freeze-drying bodies into sixty-six pound boxes of organic and nutritious powder. You place the "coffin" in the ground and overtop of it the plant or tree of your choosing (the scientist in question fancied herself coming back as a rhododendron). This, too, appeals to me. Yours truly at rest below his favourite, a white pine, his old bones becoming bone meal and nurturing the tree as it reaches for the sky.

A tree is such a capable, miraculous entity—cleansing the air, offering shade and building material, shelter for birds and creatures, beauty always, and, of course, firewood.

A Pattern Language is a classic book that some architects consider their bible. The several authors of that thick book talk about archetypes and universal truths and what makes the best buildings work. Like the fact that rooms with two windows to let in light are more likely to be used than a room with only one window. Or how "the need for fire is almost as fundamental as the need for water." They call fire "an emotional touchstone, comparable to trees, other people, a house, the sky." They quote Gaston Bachelard and his book *The Psychoanalysis of Fire*. "The fire confined to the fireplace," he writes, "was no doubt for man the first object of reverie, the symbol of repose, the invitation to repose ... to be deprived of reveries before a burning fire is to lose the first use and the truly human use of fire."

Frank Lloyd Wright, perhaps the most influential American architect of the twentieth century, believed that humans possess an instinctive need to huddle around fire, and that fire did not just warm the body but salved the soul. It seems we have forgotten the lessons of this roaring lion who condemned what he called "coffin-like houses and topless towers." (He *loathed* skyscrapers.)

Born in tiny Richland Center, Wisconsin, in 1869, Wright designed at Lake Dalton in his home state a tiny cabin built around a giant hearth, the layered stone meant to mimic the ledges on cliffs nearby. The wooden lean-to attached is unusual in that it's higher at the front and lower where it actually attaches to the cabin, giving the lean-to the look of a baseball cap with its peak snapped skyward to let in more light on the wearer's face. The cabin was Wright's last commission, in 1957, and he never lived to see its completion.

Throughout his life, Wright never lost his belief in the importance of the hearth, or, as his biographer, Meryle Secrest, put it in her book *Frank Lloyd Wright*, that "the fireplace was the primeval center, almost the high altar of the house." Wright once wrote, echoing Henry David Thoreau, "It comforted me to see the fire burning deep in the solid masonry of the house itself."

Wright was arrogant and self-possessed, and he could be prickly, but he and his architecture appeal to me in many ways.

Only when I read Secrest's book did I understand why. Wright was proud of his Welsh blood, and, like many Celts, he had a profound sense of place and an Arcadian vision of man in harmony with nature and the surrounding landscape. The Welsh traditionally saw nature as a sheltering and restoring force in the face of adversity. In his lifetime, Wright built two homes of his own called Taliesin (one in Wisconsin and one in Arizona). Taliesin was the name of a mythical Welsh poet-prophet, a name that means "shining brow," and it perhaps explains why the Wisconsin version was built into the side of a hill.

There is a curious connection in the Wright family with Abraham Lincoln and log cabins. Wright's uncle, a preacher, apparently loved to reminisce about the boyhood he spent living in a log cabin. I like Secrest's line, "He certainly was aware that no story is more powerful than the one about the little boy who begins life in a log cabin." Wright's father gave the eulogy at the funeral of Abraham Lincoln, the president most strongly affiliated with the log cabin as symbol of American pioneer spirit.

Bohemian, pacifist, visionary, Wright was the father of "organic architecture," and he had a great respect for building materials, especially local ones. He would come to believe in the beauty of small, and he never lost his conviction that true life was lived close to the soil.

One year, Henry David Thoreau installed a wood-burning stove in his cabin's fireplace. While this change made it easier to cook and to heat the little cabin, he missed staring at the fire. "I felt as though I had lost a companion," he wrote in *Walden*. "You can always see a face in the fire." This is a game I play often: bluesman B.B. King on the boom box, Dusty snoozing at my side on the couch, I gaze into the flames, looking through the glass of the woodstove for shapes—the head of a lion, the prow of a ship, a dragon's mouth—as the logs burn and crumble.

My first act upon entering the cold silent cabin in winter is the ritual preparation of the fire. It will be hours before toque and gloves and jacket are doffed. First, open stove's glass door (sound of metal hinges complaining). Clean out ash from last fire (grey cakes tumbling into the metal pail, fine dust rising). Use same ash and a damp cloth to clean the glass gone black and grey and burnt orange from previous fire, then dry to a gleaming sheen. Prepare the crumpled bed of newspaper (a newsprint addict never lacks for it) and kindling (the building of cabin, shed, and privy left a decade's supply), strike the wooden match (preferably Sea-Dog Impregnated Safety Matches Special Quality Made in Sweden), leave the door slightly ajar to boost the fire's air supply and launch the blaze, admire the sound of kindling snapping, the rush of cold cabin air into the rolling boiling fire, hear the tick of the stovepipe, watch the magnetic gauge on the pipe record the rising temperature, and wait …

The woodstove is the cabin's sole source of heat. What passes, on spring and fall evenings, for a charming and inviting diversion that also takes away the chill becomes, in the dead of winter, something else. The hearth truly becomes the beating heart of the place. The good news about log cabins is that the great mass of wood, once warm, radiates additional warmth. In the absence of a furnace, though, all that stone cold wood can take a long, long time to thaw out and start radiating anything like warmth. When I come for several days in winter, and if outside temperatures are minus twenty or colder, the cabin is finally reaching "room temperature" just about the time I am leaving it. The first few hours are the coldest; sometimes—if it's sunny—I'll go outside, for it's often milder without than within. I may let the stove do its work while I split wood (proving the adage that wood heats you thrice—on splitting, stacking, and burning) or go for a long walk with Dusty.

For esthetic reasons, the woodstove is set inside the hearth, but this limits the stove's ability to heat the space. Ideal would be a free-standing stove in the centre of the room, with a long stovepipe giving off yet more heat; such an arrangement would heat the cabin in no time. My challenge—how to convey the heat from that firebox to the cabin's far corners—is a Rube Golbergian contraption: two whisper-quiet computer fans held by vertical and horizontal stretches of piano wire in the high outside corners of the firebox.

Small and delicate (four inches by four inches and one inch thick), the fans are miraculous little feats of engineering capable of moving a lot of hot air. The one I had on hand (it served our place in Camden East, which featured its own woodstoves and heating challenges). The other I found in an alley behind a computer store, tipped off by a clerk who told me that a university student—enraged by the vagaries of his machine—had heaved the thing out his fifth-floor window the night before. It was an easy bit of mechanics to free the fan from the wreckage.

As heat pumps, the small fans work surprisingly well. Nevertheless, the hearth in severe winter cold is not a place I stray far from. The desk where I write gets pulled close, so my behind, at least, is warm (though I still long for those Dickens-style gloves with the fingers poking out). I change into what passes for my pyjamas by that fire, eat meals by that fire, read my paper on the couch in the fire's cozy embrace. Bedtime sees me armoured in sweatpants and sweatshirt with hood (a vaguely thuggish look), and I dash upstairs before leaping under the duvet, feeling a shiver or two to start, then comfort as my body heats the space beneath the covers. The last sounds I hear before drifting off are music and the fire.

On the boom box may be the sweetest sextet in the world—Miles Davis, John Coltrane, Cannonball Adderley, Bill Evans, Paul Chambers, and Jimmy Cobb. "Kind of Blue" is perhaps the most remarkable jazz album ever made. If the cabin has a theme song, it's a piece called "So What" from that miraculous collaboration. The last time I checked, sales of this music—made in 1959—had surpassed the six-million-dollar mark. On a recent jazz/blues best-seller list compiled by the Canadian recording industry, "Kind of Blue" was ranked number eight and had been on the chart for 335 weeks. Jazz critic Ashley Kahn wrote a book about the making of the album, and so I know that composer Quincy Jones plays "Kind of Blue" every day ("It's my orange juice"). That singer Shirley Horn cries every time she hears it. And that one of Davis's inspirations was time at his grandfather's farm, and, especially, walking home from church after an evening of gospel music. "That feeling is what I was trying to get close to … ," Davis once said, "six years old, walking with my cousin along that dark Arkansas road."

And for all the brilliance of the playing by Davis and Coltrane, it's the understated piano of Bill Evans I have come to hear most as I nod off. Miles Davis said Evans was the one who opened musical doors for him, that Evans—this bookish man and the only white guy in the band—had a special sound, "like crystal notes or sparkling water cascading down from some clear waterfall." Davis would sometimes call him up, Miles on the East Coast, Bill on the West, and Davis would ask Evans to lay down the phone and just play for him. An audience of one Miles three thousand miles away. It's a lovely image, one that often comes to me as "Kind of Blue" wafts up from the flame-broken darkness below.

The woodstove issues the pop and crackle of old maple. Dusty makes a lazy turn before touching down on the couch (like her ancestor, the wolf, which turns in tight circles in high grass till the bed is made), her nose pointed at the flames. She utters a heavy languid sigh and soon twitches in her sleep and begins to dream. Of chasing, and never catching, rabbits at the Point, chipmunks in the woods, deer in the field by the cabin.

Thoreau built his cabin at Walden Pond near Concord, Massachusetts, in 1845 for twenty-eight dollars and twelve cents. The fifteen-by-ten-foot cabin derived from nearby trees he cut himself, hand-split cedar roof shingles, and recycled lumber bought from Irish railway workers who had been living in local shacks. The cabin contained a writing desk, a bed, a table, and three chairs he named Solitude, Friendship, and Society. The "hermit of Walden," a Harvard graduate, had given teaching a go, then joined his father making lead pencils, but that didn't satisfy either. What did bring him joy were walks in the woods and writing about what he saw and heard and felt on those walks. They were often slow walks, saunters in emulation of the camel, the only creature, he claimed, that could simultaneously cogitate and ambulate.

Thoreau cobbled together a living by whitewashing, gardening, fence building, surveying, lecturing occasionally, and penning the odd magazine article. His *Walden, or, Life in the Woods,* became part of a literature and history that led to the cabin becoming synonymous with escape and nostalgia. Daniel Boone and Davy Crockett lived in log cabins—when they were home and not fighting Indians and bears on the frontier. (Boone had a strict concept of privacy and doubtless drove his family mad with it: his rule was that if he could see on the horizon over the treetops the smoke of a neighbour's fire, it was time to move on.) Butch Cassidy, the nineteenth-century outlaw who partnered famously with the Sundance Kid, was said to have built a log cabin. Robert Frost had a log cabin. The hewn log cabin became part of the mythology of the United States. (Less so in Canada, though our first prime minister, Sir John A. Macdonald, lived in a log house west of Kingston during his boyhood.)

The American tourist industry certainly knows the value of preserved log cabins. The cabin where Teddy Roosevelt lived while serving in the army near Medora, North Dakota, is now a historic site. Likewise the cabin in Pepin, Wisconsin, in which Laura Ingalls Wilder—author of the *Little House on the Prairie* books—lived as a child. And the log cabin that sheltered General George Washington at Valley Forge, Pennsylvania, in 1777.

Log cabin quilts—characterized by their interlocking geometric shape and strong use of rectangular (log-shaped) elements—

came into vogue at the time of the American Civil War and remain popular today. Legend has it that such quilts were hung on lines to signal safe haven for blacks fleeing slavery through the Underground Railroad.

There was even a "log cabin half dollar" with Ulysses S. Grant depicted on one side and what looks to be (but is not) a log cabin on the other. The log cabin was part of the nostalgic packaging of Honest Abe Lincoln, likewise of General Grant, Andrew Johnson, Andrew Jackson, and James Knox Polk. President William Henry Harrison was the first to capitalize, making the log cabin the symbol of his presidential campaign in 1840. One book, *From Log-Cabin to White House,* plots President James A. Garfield's rise to power and notes this peculiarity: Garfield, Lincoln, and Benjamin Harrison—log cabin presidents all—died in office. *The Log Cabin in America,* written in 1969, includes a photograph of a pre-fab miniature Daniel Boone cabin. The log cabin as playhouse.

Lincoln Logs, a children's building toy, got its patent in 1920 and featured real wood. The inventor was John Lloyd Wright, son of Frank Lloyd. The younger Wright had witnessed construction in Tokyo of his father's famous earthquake-proof Imperial Hotel and claimed this as the inspiration for the building blocks. Wright named them after Lincoln to mark the fiftieth anniversary of the end of the American Civil War and introduced the toy in 1917, at the height of the First World War. The toy was considered an appropriate, even patriotic, toy while war raged in Europe.

The Canadian variation was called Canadian Logs and featured cedar dowels of varying lengths, all notched at the corners like the real thing. I remember playing with them as a boy. We have a 1948 Eaton's catalogue at home, and there the logs are on page 514:

"You can build log cabins, forts, barns and many other items with these Logs," reads the copy, near an illustration that shows a boy in a cardigan and tie building his cabin. "Rough finished, well-fitting logs that are stained a natural colour. The more logs you have, the larger the models you can build." Makes sense. The fifty-three-piece set sold that year for one dollar and nineteen cents.

Today, readers of *Martha Stewart Living* magazine can build a "Presidents Day Log Cabin," made from a milk carton, peanut butter, pretzels, and graham crackers. And Lincoln Logs are still around, though I doubt the folks at Lego are much worried.

The pioneer cabin may make for an enticing toy or even an edible decoration, but do not romanticize nineteenth-century life. Women would lose their eyesight—never mind die young—after sewing half the night by candlelight and rising at dawn to bake bread and feed the animals.

In her book *I Come from the Valley,* Joan Finnigan keeps alive the memories of Ottawa Valley men and women who had feet in both centuries—the twentieth and the one before. The Irish who came to the valley were at first grateful for their humble digs (they were grateful to have anything to call their own). But the thin soil and hard forest were never meant to be farmed, and most of the Irish left behind what Finnigan calls "their first dwellings, charnel-house of dreams, the log cabin."

The Opeongo Trail—now part of a minor highway that runs through places in the Ottawa Valley such as Dacre and Mount St. Patrick and Renfrew—had some forty log buildings along its route as recently as 1976. This was more than any other one place in the whole province and perhaps on the continent. What had lured settlers there in the mid-1800s was the provincial government's promise—in literature aimed at would-be settlers—of "an abundance of the very best land for farming purpose." Of course, the land was, and is, all rock and lakes and timber.

By 1860, there were 941 souls on the Opeongo Road, most of them dispossessed Irish (the "pig-head Irish," as they were called) who had no choice but to try to make a go of it. "The long trail of deserted log cabins and barns," writes Finnigan, "tell a tale of struggle and disappointment. Some of these farms are still occupied and worked, and the log buildings are still in use, but many are empty, deserted, falling into ruin."

Those log houses would have gone up with much hope. Settlers were allotted land on just a few conditions—they had to be eighteen years or older, take possession within a month, cultivate a minimum of twelve acres in the next four years, maintain their share of the road, and build a house at least twenty feet by eighteen feet. A government document, *Conditions of 1860,* made it all seem cut and dried: "The log house required by the government to be built is of such a description as can be put up in four days by five men. The neighbours generally help to build the log cabin for the newly-arrived settlers without charge and when this is done, the cost of erection is small; the roof can be covered with bark, and the spaces between the logs plastered with clay and white-washed. It then becomes a neat dwelling and warm as a stone house."

Most of us look back on the famous "bees" that would raise a log house in several days as symbols of cooperative effort, neighbourliness, and community spirit. And they were. Men became adept at these endeavours: each log had to be felled, then put up and anchored in crosstrees before a chalk line was made on the round log. The log would be "scored" or made square by skilled men with broadaxes who hewed the log. "You dassn't cross the [chalk] line," remembers John King, who was born in 1895. "If you did," he told Joan Finnigan, "you weren't hewing." And once the log was set up atop another, it was cornered by what King called "professional axemen ... They tried to put on as good a corner as they could, because the building was there for keeps."

The men would have used a wide range of hand tools, some of their names and uses now all but forgotten. The menacing looking timber carrier and peavey (a pike for lifting and turning heavy logs). The draw knife (to make the logs flat). The peeling spud (for taking off bark). And all manner of axes: broadaxe, single bit axe, oxhead axe. There were adzes, augers, slicks, and bucking saws. The men whittled their own headless wooden pegs called trunnels or tree nails—made of hard and durable woods such as locust, oak, or hickory—to hold the uppermost logs in place and guard against shifting. About a dozen such pegs survived our own cabin's transition from Westport to its new location, and they occupy a place of honour on the fireplace mantel—some pegs no wider than my finger and five inches long, one eighteen inches long and as thick as my wrist. I tell people who admire them that some log houses were built by men using only a broadaxe and no hardware; the skill of such builders has largely been lost, like the words and phrases they would have bandied about.

Bird mouth described a notch in each uppermost rafter. *Hewing dogs* were iron stays driven into logs to secure them during the hewing process. A *riving horse,* similarly, supported wood during the splitting of shakes and staves. In the United States, a *thirty-penny spike* was a heavy nail that could be bought in batches of one hundred for thirty cents. *Juggles* were the heavy chips of wood cut by a broadaxe. A *dogtrot house* comprised two square or rectangular log *pens* separated by a breezeway, all under one roof and with fireplaces at either end. A *saddlebag house* was a variation on that theme: two pens under one roof with a fireplace in the middle. One *parged* and *pegged* and *pinned* and laid down *puncheons,* wielded *push poles* and *butt poles* and *gin poles,* and when all was done one had a log house or cabin that offered temporary shelter en route to something grander. And many were, indeed, temporary. But the ones that were built with care and skill still stand centuries later.

I imagine that the cabin builders were as playful as they were precise. In one old book on notching, I spotted a drawing of "a backwoods level": a mickey of fluid (rye?) laid flat against a board and secured by rounds of string at the one-quarter and three-quarters full marks. When the air bubble lodged in the middle between the two strings, the board was (more or less) at level.

At some work sites, the kind exemplified by that bracing and rallying barn-raising scene among the Amish in the Harrison Ford film *Witness,* the rye inside the backwoods level would have been safe. Less so at others. Many pioneer bees in nineteenth-century Canada ended in drunken slugfests. "A good host," wrote Richard and Janet Lunn in their history of the county where the cabin now sits, "was a man who never minded his guests fighting … Fights were harsh, dangerous and often fatal. Men, in their cups, would lose tempers on barn roofs and rafters, fall and break their necks. It was almost expected that someone would be killed or seriously injured at every barn-raising." When, prior to a logging bee, a woman set up a long table in her yard, her twelve-year-old daughter was incredulous. "Where," she asked, "are the men going to fight?"

The men would be divided into teams of four, each with two oxen, and they would race each other in their labour, with a "grog boss" ladling out whiskey along the way. They would work till midday, then eat a huge meal "washed down with lashings of tea and whiskey," as Una Abrahamson notes in her *God Bless Our Home: Domestic Life in Nineteenth Century Canada*. They worked till dusk, whereupon another great meal was consumed, the cut log ends would be tossed into a bonfire, and all would gather to roast corn, tell ghost stories, and dance—often until dawn. At which point work would recommence. "Many men," says Abrahamson, "thought it lucky to be the first to straddle the cross-beam of the roof." I wonder how many fell to their deaths from fatigue and the hard cheap liquor that coursed in them.

Drunkenness was the great scourge of the nineteenth century, and the temperance movement fought a losing battle against it. Whiskey was cheap and ubiquitous: most medicines of the day contained rum or gin, and steady customers at the general store were often rewarded with a free drink. And, notes Abrahamson, "Spirits helped counteract the cold, the hard life, the loneliness and the boredom."

And the darkness of their cabins. Pioneer cabins had either no windows or a few tiny ones; they would be boarded up in winter and in summer covered with oiled paper, newspaper, or animal skin. Glass was expensive, and pioneers would learn a hard truth about single-pane windows: they let light in and heat out. And though heat and light were both deemed precious, the former would have been seen as necessity, the latter mere luxury. Some cabin dwellers resorted to greased paper or rows of empty pickle jars. In the stifling heat of summer, doors would be left open and mosquitoes, bed bugs, fleas, flies, and hornets had the run of the place. Charles Dickens called the log cabins he saw in the United States during a visit in 1842 dark and brooding, "utterly forlorn and miserable … squalid to the last degree."

Alexis de Tocqueville, the French historian who had toured the United States a decade or so earlier, was nevertheless impressed by log cabins. In his classic *Democracy in America,* he commented on how the open concept of the log house gathered the entire family and buttressed them against the wilderness. "This dwelling forms as it were a little world of its own. It is an ark of civilization … a sort of oasis in the desert. A hundred paces beyond it the everlasting forest stretches its shades around it and solitude begins again."

He was right about the cabin as oasis. A nineteenth-century visitor to Canada, George Head wrote *Forest Scenes and Incidents, in the Wilds of North America; Being a Diary of a Winter's Route from Halifax to the Canadas, and During Four Months' Residence in the Woods on the Borders of Lakes Huron and Simcoe.* He described in detail the log cabin hospitality he experienced in the 1820s. Every cabin was seen as a possible refuge, for few inns then existed.

The great generosity of the day bordered on obligation, for to turn away a man in winter often meant death for that traveller.

Many pioneer homes featured a wooden latch on the inside of the door, which could be lifted from the outside by a leather latch-string that passed through a hole in the door. The owner could, of course, pull in the string at night, but generally it was left out; an expression arose—"the latch-string is always out." Imagine leaving the key in the front door of your house along with a sign, "All Visitors Welcome," and you get an idea of pioneer hospitality.

The result, Head wrote, was that "a man cannot be said to be master of his own house … he cannot … walk across his bedroom after nine o'clock at night without the risk of disturbing some great fellow stretched out and snoring before his fire, and who, if he happen to be trodden upon, will swear as loudly as if the whole house belonged to him." One night, Head shared a cabin no larger than mine with thirty-six people and eight large dogs. The cabins were hot, their inhabitants tormented by fleas, and, since there were rarely partitions, the cabins were also impossibly noisy. Crying babies, barking dogs, and, of course, snoring men and women.

Still, given the alternative—sleeping outside in the bone-rattling, killing cold—the weary traveller in the bush must have seen the light in the window of a log house as a welcome sight. "Although the dwelling of a Canadian peasant may not deserve much praise," Head wrote, "too much cannot be said of his fire." Enormous logs—requiring the strength of two or three men to move them—would be laid in the cabin's huge fireplaces. The French called such a log *le bûche* and it would burn for up to forty-eight hours.

Susanna Moodie, for her part, had no great love for the pioneer log cabin—not at first anyway. In *Roughing It in the Bush, or, Forest Life in Canada,* she describes early on being driven in a wagon to their first abode. The driver pointed to "a miserable hut at the bottom of a steep descent … I gazed upon the place in perfect dismay, for I had never seen such a shed called a house before."

"You must be mistaken," she told the driver, "that is not a house but a cattle-shed, or pig-sty." The driver told her she had much to learn. An "untenable tenement" she called it. "The prospect was indeed dreary. Without, pouring rain; within, a fireless hearth; a room with but one window, and that containing only one whole pane of glass." They sat in the room, devoid of furniture and even a door (it was found on the ground outside) and proceeded to set about "abusing the place, the country, and our own dear selves for our folly in coming to it." My folly had nothing on Susanna's.

Nor was she enamoured of the logging bee. These gatherings, Moodie wrote, "are considered indispensable, and much has been written in their praise; but to me, they represent the most disgusting picture of a bush life. They are noisy, riotous, drunken meetings, often terminating in violent quarrels, sometimes even in bloodshed." Thirty-two men gathered at their bee and worked for free, but Moodie was convinced that paying two or three good (sober) men would have seen them further ahead.

A ditty of the day, credited to John Dunbar Moodie—Susanna's husband—and memorialized in her *Roughing It in the Bush,* went like this:

There was a man in our town,
In our town, in our town—
There was a man in our town,
He made a logging bee;
  And he bought lots of whisky,
  To make the loggers frisky—
  To make the loggers frisky,

    At his logging bee.

The Devil sat on a log heap,
A log heap, a log heap—
A red-hot burning log heap—
A-grinning at the bee;
  And there was lots of swearing,
  Of boasting and of daring,
  Of fighting and of tearing,

    At that logging bee.

Moodie's book is a near constant whine, and though at times she seems enthralled by the sight and sound of running water, her last sentence reads like a warning sign posted on the dark and lonely road to a haunted house. "If these sketches should prove the means of deterring one family from sinking their property, and shipwrecking all their hopes, by going to reside in the backwoods of Canada, I shall consider myself amply repaid for revealing the secrets of the prison-house, and feel that I have not toiled and suffered in the wilderness in vain."

In one of her other books, *Life in the Clearings versus the Bush,* Moodie includes a poem called "The Canadian Herd-Boy," with its line "On all around deep silence broods." The woods made her fearful, the cabin offered a poor sort of refuge, and clearly she was witness to more sorrow and deprivation than hers alone. *Life in the Clearings* includes some wrenching stories of small children wandering off paths in the woods and never being seen again. Two boys, five and seven, take lunch to their father in the woods, wander off the path, and one boy is never found. A girl following her father on a road between their shanty and a sawmill is tempted into the bush by wildflowers, finds herself lost, and does the sensible thing: she sits under a tree, says a prayer, and waits to be found, which she was.

Moodie's sister Catharine Parr Traill, on the other hand, was an optimist by nature and took a lifelong interest in the botany of the new world. The books in her library were stuffed with leaves and ferns and flowers she had collected and pressed. Her collected letters to a sister in England formed the basis of her book *Lost in the Backwoods: A Tale of the Canadian Forest.* As Charlotte Gray put it in *Sisters in the Wilderness,* Traill's "sunny personality almost leaps off every page." The sisters endured all manner of tragedy—fire, near ceaseless deprivation, the untimely deaths of some of their children—yet Catharine, at least, never lost her sense that the very land that buffetted them could comfort them too. In 1899, when Catharine was ninety-seven years old, her daughter Kate took her to Minnewawa, Kate's cottage on Stony Lake—familiar territory to the old woman. That summer, and over her daughter's protests, she would take her cherrywood staff and gingerly explore the woods behind the cottage looking for flowers and berries. Catharine would sit on the shaded porch and cast crumbs to the birds and watch canoes breeze past. She loved, Kate says in Gray's book, "the wild and picturesque rocks, trees, hill and valley, wild-flowers, ferns, shrubs and moss and the pure sweet scent of pines over all, breathing health and strength. 'If I were a doctor,' she had once written, 'I would send my patients to live in a shanty under the pines.'"

Catharine Parr Traill's interest in nature reflected her questing spirit, which was both deeply spiritual and relentlessly scientific. She believed that nature was proof of God's touch and goodness, and though the seasons could be savage, she took delight in them. "The pines were now putting on their rich, mossy, green spring dresses," she wrote in *Canadian Crusoes.* Yet she was also intensely keen to know the plant's life cycle, its value as food and medicine, and its broader place in botany.

When Charlotte Gray, as part of her research for *Sisters in the Wilderness,* perused Traill's old scrapbooks, now held in the archives of the Museum of Nature in Ottawa, Gray marvelled at what she found between those decaying pages: red lichens, the purple blossoms of fireweed, pressed sphagnum and ferns "anchored on white birch bark and decorated with faded maple leaves," and, finally, "tiger moths, their delicate wings flaking with age, and the orange feathers of a northern oriole." Who can read this and not be touched? How did Catharine find time for this? More to the point, why can't we find time for this?

Traill came to Canada with her husband in 1832, when the cabin I now call mine had been up a mere five years. One has to wonder how many other women have read Traill's books and taken inspiration from them, for more than a few have found solace by being alone in a remote cabin.

In 1914, Laura Lee Davidson—a teacher from Baltimore in her mid-forties—decided to spend a winter alone in a cottage on an island on Bob's Lake near Westport, Ontario (the original site, remember, of the Bresee cabin). "I am tired to death," she wrote in *A Winter of Content*. "Instead of the clang of car bells and the honk of automobile horns, I want to hear the winds sing across the ice fields, instead of the smell of asphalt and hot gasoline, I want the odour of wet earth in boggy places. I have loved the woods all my life; I long to see the year go round there just once before I die."

Davidson was dropped off at the end of the summer. She had enough food, supplies, and wood put away to let her endure till the following spring. As she would later report, the experience transformed her. "It has given me health," she wrote. "I sleep all night like a stone; I eat plain food with relish; I walk and row mile after mile; I work rejoicing in my strength and glad to be alive." Davidson also remarked on a dramatic shift in priorities; things she once took for granted—"like air and sunshine, warm fires and the kind faces of friends—are now the most valuable things in the world."

What held true for this woman almost a century ago seems just as valid today, maybe more so. In his book *Escape: In Search of the Natural Soul of Canada*, Roy MacGregor describes taking out an ad in *Cottage Life* magazine to test a hypothesis. It is the one that powers his book—that the promise of escape, even temporary escape, to our cottages and cabins and retreats is what makes frenetic life in the city bearable for many Canadians. One of MacGregor's correspondents was a woman who described her own therapy—a cabin deep in the bush without running water, electricity, phone, or even cooking stove. The cabin, the woman wrote MacGregor, "is my respite ... my escape from all the routines and obligations of urban life. I escape from protecting my kids from cars and strangers, walking my dog who can run free, noise, pollution, cars, neighbours, phone calls, faxes, shopping, laundry ... the list is endless."

What impresses about MacGregor's witnesses is how devoted and dedicated they are to their sanctuaries. One Calgary geologist lives nine hours by plane and car—a 2,177-mile haul—from the family cottage in Ontario; yet they go there five times a year. Some families posted overseas take the same trouble to get back to their northern retreats. Such places, MacGregor writes, "had kept their sanity, preserved their marriage, and, in several cases, even returned them to sobriety."

This is the power of a little downtime in a place removed. John Muir, the Scottish émigré to the United States who founded the Sierra Club, died the year that Laura Lee Davidson wintered on that island. "Wilderness," he proclaimed in *Our National Parks,* "is a necessity" for "tired, nerve-shaken, over-civilized people." Muir had found in nature, and especially his family's eighty-acre farm by the Fox River in Wisconsin, respite from a cruel and sadistic father. "Everybody," Muir maintained, "needs beauty as well as bread, places to play in and pray in, where Nature may heal and cheer and give strength to body and soul."

In his book *A Separate Place,* published in 2000, David Brill describes how the small cabin he helped build on sixty-eight acres of riverfront wilderness in Tennessee gave him strength to forge a new relationship with his young daughters and come to terms with the end of his marriage. The experience convinced him that "time spent in reflection and retreat—retreat to mountaintops, to shorelines, to monasteries, to quiet rooms with soft chairs—is not time wasted," that nature is both a divine and infallible guide.

Brill, it transpires, is a teacher, and one of his colleagues who had arranged to work from her own cabin in the Appalachian Mountains had warned him that the cabin would soon exert a powerful tug on him. "You'll count the hours until Friday afternoon and your departure for the cabin," she said. "And you'll cry every Sunday night when you have to come back." And Brill did find it difficult to close up the cabin and head for a home that was far more bitter than sweet. Eventually, though, he would conclude that the best hope for staying connected to the world is a little disconnect now and again. "Those who leave," he wrote, "who go to a separate place, no matter how remote, no matter how long their stay, will return to the world enriched, healed and empowered ..."

Even teenagers battling for their lives seem to find sustenance in nature. Dr. Sylvain Baruchel, a pediatric oncologist at the Hospital for Sick Children in Toronto, helps direct a national (and soon to become international) program that sends young cancer patients from across Canada on northern expeditions to canoe and hike and camp in the wild. It's called On the Tip of the Toes Foundation, and Dr. Baruchel is one of its founders. Cancer treatment often deals terrible blows to the self-esteem of sensitive teenagers who see their hair fall out, their weight balloon, their usual strength and balance disappear following radiation and chemotherapy. These northern expeditions—to James Bay and Ellesmere Island and other destinations—present enormous challenges at the best of times, more so for these weakened teens. But canoeing rapids, hauling gear over long portages, camping in sometimes dramatic weather, forming alliances with others who face the same threat and the same harsh medical treatments, the wilderness itself—all serve to revive and restore.

What seems to make "adventure therapy" work is simply getting away from it all. And while the early studies merely suggest the benefits of such escape, about two-thirds of participants apparently believe themselves to be better off after these trips than before. One young man with incurable brain cancer could barely walk as the trip to Ellesemere Island began, but by the end he was playing soccer on a northern beach. Nature heals, he told Dr. Baruchel. "Nature is medicine."

A similar vein of pantheism runs through Jake MacDonald's book *Houseboat Chronicles: Notes from a Life in Shield Country*. This ex–altar boy become fishing guide and writer understands perfectly when a marketing executive with Ontario Tourism describes his findings after polling twenty-seven thousand American anglers. Asked to list their top ten reasons for coming to Canada, the respondents put at the top "'experiencing the beauty of nature.' Most of them, in other words," wrote MacDonald, "were trying to connect with God … and fishing was their cover story."

Sigurd Olson, the writer and noted conservationist who often led such trips into the Minnesota wilderness, was arguing in the 1950s that wilderness canoe trips had a profound healing effect on his clients. It's still true. One contemporary researcher surveyed the psychological impact on participants of one hundred wilderness trips, and the overwhelming and consistent result was stress reduction. Civilized man, Olson had argued, needs the spiritual and physical nourishment that the wild offers, and many people go there "once a month or once a year as a sick man might go to his physician."

In the summer of 2003, I attended a wedding held in front of a friend's remote (and solar-powered) cabin on the shores of Lillooet Lake three hours north of Vancouver. That morning the rains had finally ceased and blue sky declared itself, a complement to the aquamarine green of the lake, the Lincoln green of the mountains in the foreground, and the white of the snow that still capped jagged Mount Garibaldi in the background. The beauty was surreal.

I played the role of the doubting Thomas from the east. "They're fake," I said of the mountains. "It's a trick with mirrors." The wedding party had aligned themselves on the lawn with that glorious vista behind them.

Later, I fell into a conversation with a wedding guest named Cliff, who lived with his wife year-round in a cabin close by. Now in his early sixties, he said he had been an alcoholic until he was thirty-five when a wilderness retreat rescued him. He would witness many such transformations on other retreats into nature and even meet his wife, Diana, on one. Cliff spoke of the quiet on Lillooet Lake, how time here goes on bringing him peace. I had the sense of an intensely spiritual man. "This," Cliff said on the lawn that day, pointing out aross the water of the lake, "is my cathedral."

To which Traill and Brill and Davidson et al. would have said, Amen.

Meanwhile, back at the cabin, I am like the gardener who digs up plants every spring and relocates them, according to colour and height and whim. In my case, I'm shifting around old timbers. The two four-by-four pillars that support the hammock and the three like pillars that frame the solar shower—all once served as roof beams in the original Bresee log house. Those five beams are weathered now, their muted brown a counter to the massive grey beams of the cabin. Like cousins, they all seem cut from the same cloth.

The roof beams were sawn in 1827 and when you trim their brothers, as I did one fall, I noticed that they still emit a fresh smell. As sweet as baby's breath. One roof beam still bears the lettering N6 in black (North 6, I presume), more proof that the log house was dismantled by the Atchesons before Connor and company took it apart. Connor's lads had piled the roof beams on wooden pallets to the north of the cabin while Connor tried to convince Michael and me that the beams were owed a second life supporting our new roof. We'd even save some money. Michael would have none of it, nor surely would the building inspector, who was never given the chance to scoff at the suggestion. The building code, I came to believe, was my friend, and there was no code in 1827. My enemy was romantic ideas about old wood, and it felt good to resist what I am prey to.

I thought of all this one fall day as I plucked rusty square-headed nails, hundreds of them, from the old roof beams. Sometimes I'd use a piece of lumber beneath my hammer as leverage, the way Michael had taught me. The beams had been piled on skids and though they had been out in the weather for years, they were above the ground and the damp. They still felt solid and heavy, and whatever old saw had cut them, they were straight and true.

Under the heat of a belligerent sun, I pulled nails. One of the pleasures of the place is hard work, physical work, and I would wish it on all who seek to embrace a place and make it their own. The sweat dripped from my brow as I yanked and yanked. Casually, I tossed a now nail-free beam onto the new pile I was making by the woodshed; the beam snapped in two. It had *looked* fit on the outside; the dry rot and punk had lain hidden within. The mere thought of that beam being asked to help hold up our roof gave me a chill.

The ten beams that did pass muster will be given a lighter task. They will form an arbour pointing to the southwest where, one day, a pond will take shape. And so it goes at the cabin; one thing (sometimes, one damn thing) leads to another.

The oppressive heat that summer had led me to think of shade. A pergola would do the trick while the linden and maple trees we planted grew taller and wider. A country arbour, Leigh Seddon once wrote in an old issue of *Harrowsmith,* "achieves an enchanting symbiosis—the frame provides climbing plants with a foothold as they reach toward the sun, and the foliage, in turn, transforms the bare structure into a living wall and ceiling."

I would lie awake at night that fall (when my city is noisiest, as university students return and begin their assaults on their livers) and dream pergolas. Dimensions: twenty feet by fifteen feet. Beams four inches by four inches and eight feet tall, crosspieces two-inch-by-six-inch eastern white cedar, one foot apart. Lattice overtop and on the east, south, and west walls. For greenery, I would move the Virginia creeper that had serendipitously taken root by the south wall of the tool shed and flourished there, its tendrils shooting to the roof and even snaking inside the shed a little ominously like something from *The Day of the Triffids.* The creeper would be a good choice, for the early colonists had used it to grace their fences and walls, and it grows everywhere—especially at the Point. Virginia creeper would be joined by fox grapes, Boston ivy, American bittersweet, clematis. Leaves and vines and blossoms would commingle to form a dense canopy.

I would gather flat fieldstones here and there to make a stone patio under the arbour, with single rocks set in the ground on a circular path to the cabin. From spring through summer and fall, cabin to pergola would be a favoured trail on these grounds. Then pergola to pond, pond to screened-in gazebo. Each little dream led to another.

And under the arbour I would sit, admiring the dappled shade of my own making, maybe leaning against a beam that James Atcheson or a helper had cut when Canada's first prime minister was a boy of twelve.

Inserting the six vertical pieces into their new homes in the ground took most of a day, one of those bright, clear days between summer and fall. David and I would lift the heavy mechanical auger (imagine a heavy drill powered by a chainsaw engine) onto each appointed place, start the thing up, and hope for no rock. Striving for four-foot holes, we settled that first time for a depth of three feet. This looked easy enough; the heavy bit's journey through the soil was steady as she goes. But the other five holes proved progressively more troublesome, and several times I found myself rolling in the grass as if some wrestler had tossed me across a canvas ring.

Auger physics are such that as long as the drill encounters only earth, the bit will continue to rotate and cast up mounds of dirt—much like worms or ants do, though on a grander scale. But the second the auger meets rocks, even seemingly inconsequential ones, all that energy is reversed and transferred instantly to the auger's U-shaped handles. I learned to keep knees and elbows clear of this crazed mechanical bronc. It was a long day of lifting the auger out of the hole, lying flat on the ground to scoop out earth and rock with bare hands (while a certain canine licked my face), plunking the auger back in, and repeating the process many more times until the *thunk* of a flat expanse of rock, or the smell and drone of the engine, or sheer fatigue, or all of the above declared that whatever depth we had achieved by that point would have to do. Frost line be damned. By day's end, my shoulders ached, my back was stiff, and my hands were numb from auger wrestling and concrete mixing, for each post would be secured by a necklace of cement from the bottom of the hole up to soil level.

The effect of the posts on the landscape was profound. The instant you stepped out the cabin's south door, the eye was drawn to it, whatever *it* was. Some sort of Stonehenge seemed to be in the making, the neighbours might muse, or perhaps a triumphal arch. Whatever shape the gateway would take, there was no doubting that it led to the southwest corner of the field. Something else was slated for there. Where once was only field, there was now a focus.

That night the moon was full, and, like horses on which it has the same effect, I was restless and unable to sleep. We animals are mostly water, and just as the moon rules the tides, it rules some of us. Nights like this, I lean on the sill of the south-facing window and marvel at the moon. Only at the cabin do I assiduously follow the passages of the moon, see its slow rise over The Three Sisters, watch it take up a favoured perch overtop Jen's barn, then slide on its course across the black southern sky.

Throughout the night I kept sliding out of bed and staring out the west-facing window by my pillow, pleased already by the posts and their shadows in the moonlit field. In my mind's eye I was already into the next phase, lopping off the posts at an even eight feet, setting more beams atop them. I could see the crosspieces, could see the jaunty angle of the cut ends and the little pyramids and circles I would notch and drill into them. I could even see the pond, the lilies and the reeds and the wild grasses at its edge, could hear the frogs boasting and that first coyote call announcing to all within range that a little lake had miraculously appeared down by the old pioneer cabin.

Charles B. Seib has a pond of his own and a place that bears a striking resemblance to mine. In his book *The Woods: One Man's Escape to Nature,* written in 1971, this "harried newspaper editor" (at the old *Washington Evening Star,* which ceased publication in 1981) describes finding his thirty-three-acre retreat in the Virginia countryside after a six-month search. He called it, simply, The Woods, and his affection for his land seems rooted in all the labour he alone dedicated to building his shelter.

Shelter is the right word. The stained board-and-batten cabin set amid the trees alongside a half-acre pond is a spartan sixteen-by-twenty-foot room. No plumbing, no electricity, no telephone. His children called the place Walden South—for its pond, for its owner-built cabin, and for the powerful Thoreauvian impulse that led Seib to build it over the course of thirty-nine weekends between 1966 and 1969.

I have seen pictures of Seib's cabin. The roof is peaked, the heavy supporting beams exposed on the inside, with pots and pans arrayed in one corner, and a kind of jailhouse bunk set by one window and held in place by two links of chain. The cabin has the look and feel of a neat hunt camp, with a Coleman lantern strung by rope from one beam offering light, and the Franklin stove offering heat. And, like Thoreau, Seib calls its small fire "companionable."

The Woods, the book, that is, contains Seib's answer to the inevitable question: Why? "What prompts a city man with a demanding and stimulating job, a fine family, and a comfortable home to search out a private place, to assume the burden of paying for it, and then to undertake the task of building his retreat? What is there that makes him almost weekly, over a period of years, get up before dawn on his day off, drive 85 miles, work like a man possessed, and then drive back, declaring himself renewed, rested, ready to face again the pressures, frustrations, and terrors of the world he lives in?"

Seib's answers made sense to me, for they are pretty much my answers too. He was a newspaper guy writing in 1971 out of Washington. I happened to be in his city that year—marching, with a lot of other young longhairs, on the seat of power to protest the war in Vietnam. I will never forget the image of thousands of candles burning on the black wrought-iron fence around the White House, the ring of blue-uniformed police, us with our arms linked and singing peace songs. "The killing continues," Seib writes of the time, "the college kids grow increasingly bitter, the cities fester."

There is no way for a Washington newspaper editor to duck the news, and the news gathered was—and remains—invariably bad. Seib felt the desire, "childish, perhaps," to turn his back on all that—even if only for a while. He needed to reassure himself that "some things still are." That spring had come to the meadow, that the wild strawberries, the sumac, the daisies and Queen Anne's lace grew in profusion. Seib was sure there was satisfaction to be had in what Henry Beston had called "elemental things"—like fire and earth. In his book *The Outermost House,* published in 1928, Beston was insisting that "the world today is sick to its thin blood for lack of elemental things, for fire before the hands, for water welling from the earth, for air, for the dear earth itself underfoot." Seib would have added to that list working with his hands, with its "old satisfactions and verities."

Seib would go to The Woods alone and find peace in his solitude. He would revel in the quiet, find new things to discover, and even, for a minute or two, get lost in the pines of his small acreage. And he would toil at an even pace, pouring concrete for footings, cutting timbers by hand, then end his day with a swim in the pond "and a lazy hour of floating on an air mattress in the sun, contemplating the treetops and marvelling at my good fortune." By degrees, this rather ordinary property—lacking in spectacular views or stunning topography—became truly his and he would come to feel an overwhelming desire to protect it. *Stewardship* is such a fine and worthy word, but it starts with connecting with the land by working on that land. (Postscript: Charles Seib died on October 28, 2003, at the age of eighty-four.)

A first book by an amateur and self-taught woodworker made a minor splash in 2001. Tiny, at 186 pages, Ross A. Laird's *Grain of Truth: The Ancient Lessons of Craft* left its mark on this reader.

Laird is a clinical psychologist and a poet with a nice grasp of life as journey. The book kept coursing back to themes and ideas—some of them ancient—that not only made utter good sense but helped me understand my own powerful feeling for my old pioneer cabin. Words like *ritual* and *solitude, labour* and *stillness* seemed all bound up with other words: *heal, sustain, comfort.*

Laird and his wife have a cabin in south-central British Columbia. "It's not an ambitious building," he writes, "just a few hundred square feet of cinder block, tongue-and-groove fir panelling, and a roof buttressed by modest beams." It sounds a sister cabin to Seib's, and mine. What Laird feels there is a sense of place and belonging, and connection in every sense of that word. A massive brick fireplace helps make it "a welcoming cabin," and Laird describes seeing fading pencil marks on beams and feeling a kinship with the first-generation Italian immigrants who made those marks. I feel the same pull from the past when I touch a big timber marked N6 or W3 or feel the adze mark left in the wood by an Atcheson or his helper almost two centuries ago.

Ross Laird is intrigued by Taoism, the five-thousand-year-old Chinese philosophy whose sages lived in remote places doing simple physical work. Taoist sages, Laird writes, would go to quiet, removed places in the mountains or valleys—"specific sites of sacred contemplation … It was always from a secure foundation that they leapt into the unknown." And he quotes the *I Ching:*

"It is beneficial to have somewhere to go." To what Laird calls "a place of solace and refuge."

Grain of Truth is a paean to craftsmanship, to working with wood, to taking the time to do a job well. Not much happens in the book: the author makes a wooden urn to house a relative's ashes, he restores a dinghy, makes a night lantern. And not without incident, either; he lays on too much glue, mismeasures, and frets that each project will end badly. In one comic moment, he describes climbing to a rise to cut down a tree, which rolls down the hill and almost crushes his car.

But in Laird's world, quiet is a virtue, going slow beats going fast, and stillness is a lofty goal. A walk in the woods stirs awe and wonder and a profound sense of discovery; the smell of red cedar and wood shavings proves as alluring as perfume. But always, Laird comes back to this conviction that working with one's hands is joyful, restorative work.

The message of the book was one I had already embraced. Every Thanksgiving at the cabin, my ample family draw names from a hat. We had long ago ceased the practice of giving every sibling a gift at Christmas; you give only to that person whose name you have plucked. But a year ago I pushed for an amendment: the gift should not be bought, but made by the giver's own hands. The idea met with some opposition (though my mother was a keen and early backer) for execution seemed daunting to all of us. That year, with my son's help, I made a compost bin of western red cedar for my mother.

The following year I made a soapbox, a gag gift for a brash and funny Irish brother-in-law who has no trouble at all being heard above the Scanlan madding crowd. As I made the box, I could see him standing on it in the rec room of the family homestead in Scarborough on Christmas Eve, demanding to be heard while everyone in the family—to his and our delight—hurls abuse at him as if he were some bearded philosopher king targeted by hecklers in Hyde Park on a Sunday morning. The soapbox was modelled fairly precisely on an old soft drink box ("Wilson's, since 1875" it reads); I use it to house my chainsaw oil, helmet, and extra chains.

I chose ash to make the box, the same tough hardwood used for baseball bats and hockey sticks, canoe paddles and snowshoes, the same wood that grows in abundance in our forest and whose leaf juice relieves the itching and swelling of mosquito bites. The grain is subtle and pale, yellow and brown, the marks close and irregular, like the lines on a topographical map when a steep incline is indicated. A cabinetmaker might look at some of my cuts (my old jigsaw laboured through that dense wood) and shake his or her head. Ulrike, for one, knows a straight cut from a curved one. There would be no delicate mortises or tenons, no dovetail or dado joints in this apprentice's project; counter-sunk deck screws hidden under wood filler held the thing together.

But Laird was right about the contentment that comes with running sandpaper up and down the grain and feeling the wood come up softer to the touch every time. It's a bit like grooming a horse, or the tea ceremony. There is pleasure to be had in practised movement.

My simple soapbox, heavier and sturdier than need be, nonetheless gave me great satisfaction and I almost hated to part with it. I determined to make another for the cabin.

Where my simple carpentry continued. I made a firewood box, a kind of lean-to attached to the west side of the tool shed. Actually, I made the thing twice. The first model looked, and was, far too small for all the firewood in need of shelter.

"Didn't you draw up a plan?" asked Ulrike, incredulous.

"No," I said. "Just started building." I had an image in my head of what it might look like, but details—and dimensions—were fuzzy. My style is to attack with fervour. Like a man possessed, like someone in love, like the forechecker I used to be on the ice. I gave the wood cradle a floor, sides, and backing of available lumber and an angled roof of new pine boards so that the rain would sluice away, and thereby created a proper home for firewood that heretofore had occupied the same spot but with only a makeshift covering of plywood held more or less fast by wood stumps. I must be a simple man; it pleased me perhaps more than it should have to see the cradle take shape over the course of two days and to fill it to the brim with firewood. The squirrel had socked away his winter's supply of nuts and was now smug as all get-out. And every time I'd use some firewood, I'd immediately replenish it. The woodbox showed best when full.

The joyful part of working with my hands has indeed sunk in; Laird's message of going slow, of tackling the task meticulously, these lessons are slower to acquire. My instinct is to race to completion, to sup on the pleasure of a job done, thus denying myself the greater pleasure of a job well done. And I may never be anything more than a carpenter's apprentice, any more than I'll ever be anything more than an ordinary equestrian. I am, though, a work in progress, convinced more than ever that work sustains and that progress is, indeed, being made.

Perhaps craft is too pure a notion for some. They may warm to the idea of a sanctuary in a field or woods but lack the skill or patience or cash (or all three) to fashion something elegant and lasting. They want it simple, cheap, now. And I would tell them the story of The Dari-Dip.

Peter, the brother of my pal David, was first among us to set down roots in the county. Almost twenty-five years ago, he and his family bought, as a summer and weekend place, a century-old farmhouse on a narrow four-acre piece of land that fronted on a quiet road and stretched down to a rocky shelf of shoreline on Lake Ontario. At the time, Toronto was home; now Peter and Bonnie live in the county in that old (and vastly improved) red-brick house. Ulrike and I bunked there often, before and after Kurt was born. A photograph in an old family album captures the time. I have that narrowed look of one just wakened, and all five of Peter and David's kids have surrounded me on the pullout couch. They're all smiling for they know what's coming and I'm pretending not to. The next frame, had there been one, would have captured five-on-one wrestling.

It was here, in the joy of that house, that a seed was planted in the minds of David and Claudine, and Ulrike and me. We, too, would want a place in the county. In the meantime, Peter's place at Salmon Point (also known as Wicked Point) became a cherished spot to visit and, for David, to write. In 1983, while driving on county back roads—then, and still, common sport for him—he noticed a For Sale sign affixed to a building once used to dispense ice cream. It looked like a Dairy Queen box built in the 1950s, with a near flat overhanging roof to shelter customers and sliding glass windows at the front where people would have lined up for their sundaes and shakes and cones. The owners wanted two thousand dollars for The Dari-Dip, as its sign proclaimed, and David immediately realized its potential as a writer's shack. He had even, with Peter and Bonnie's blessing, picked out a spot for it below the farmhouse in the maple glen that led down to the lake.

David called house movers in Belleville, and they quoted him a price of three thousand dollars to move The Dip the eight miles to Salmon Point.

"But that's more than I paid for the building," David complained.

"Then it probably ain't worth movin'," came the reply.

Finally, David landed in the capable hands of Russell Cole, a county man in his fifties. "He was a big rangy guy," David recalls. "He looked like a cowboy. Lean and mean and gruff, but he was actually very nice." Though not one to be trifled with. Cole had apparently once been employed to move some septic tanks from a trailer park when the owner—let's call him Bert—defaulted on payments. The tanks were sitting on the ground inside a huge domed building, the kind of "igloo" often used by municipal roads departments to house sand, salt, and snowplows. But once Russell was inside, Bert locked him in and could be heard laughing as he did so, whereupon Russell got in his truck and drove right through the wall. The story ends there, so you'll have to imagine the fate of Bert. I see him landing, by means of a fist, against a septic tank.

Wearing a Pickseed ball cap and a Mickey Mouse muscle shirt, Russell Cole approached The Moving of The Dip with only these tools: a giant tow truck, eight sizeable truck jacks, logs, pipes, and wooden blocks, and a homemade flatbed trailer. By degrees, he slowly lifted The Dari-Dip into the air and then slid the trailer underneath, lowering the building by lowering each jack one notch at a time. There must have been endless, even dizzying, circling of The Dip, Cole like a predator moving slowly round and round formidable prey, cocky and wary at the same time. His helpers were his daughter, her fiancé, and a runaway boy "who had washed up on his shore," as David put it. A police escort conveyed them all the way to Peter's place, where The Dip was gently lowered onto a recently prepared concrete foundation.

"Is it pointed at the lake just right?" the man in the muscle shirt asked David.

"Not quite."

At this, Russell Cole jammed a crowbar into one of the lead pipes he had placed under each corner of the building, put one shoulder into the side of The Dip and swung it around till it was, indeed, pointed at the lake just right. At the southern edge of the oversized concrete pad, five little hands had made their marks when the goo was still wet. The five cousins—Arwyn, Robbie, Harry, Hadley, and Reeves—had left their signatures, and though The Dip is gone now the concrete pad is still there, as are the handprints. Green mould lends them the dignity of gargoyles in an English garden, but the sight of them makes me happy and sad at the same time, for the kids would have giggled as they laid their palms in the softness and I can almost conjure the sounds of their sweet glee.

The cost to move the building: three hundred dollars. Years later, Russell Cole was summoned back to scoop up The Dip. His prices had risen only marginally: to three hundred and seventy-five dollars. The Dip, you see, was only temporary, and so, it turns out, was David and Claudine's marriage. The thirty-year union came asunder in the spring of 2002, their land across the road from our cabin was sold in a matter of days, and our dreams of the Wicked Point Winery came undone (though someone else's more ambitious vineyard would follow). The land fell into new hands, as did its centrepiece, the forest that some still call "Web's bush," after the former owner who fussed over it mightily. Like the fastidious horseman who caught manure before it landed in the stalls, Web—or so the story goes—caught dead twigs and branches before they touched the ground.

David and Claudine, inspired by our cabin, had picked out a spot near Web's bush where we all believed a house would one day go. I had planted several dozen white pines at the site, and David had proudly planted a nursery maple there. Shade for the house of their dreams. The picnic table was hauled out to mark the spot, and I remember the four of us—Ulrike, Claudine, David, and I—sitting on it, having a beer on a summer's day, laughing. I remember David on the riding lawn mower he called Wayne. Claudine planting flowers in her shade garden under the bower near the vines, wrapping delicate white lights at the arched entryway, digging for the little pond she wanted by the bench. David and I would joke about a grey-haired tomorrow, about having barns and horses, about ritual rides to the Point to watch the sun drop into the lake.

By mid-summer, Claudine's garden was besieged by weeds and grass, and the wind had overturned and crumpled the wooden swing. I would go there in the evening and cut flowers for vases in the cabin and walk through the woods—along a sugar maple path that Dusty and I knew well. By fall, I couldn't bear to go back and never went again. None of this seemed even remotely possible in the days of The Dip.

One lesson of The Dip is clear. With a little gumption and a little luck, you can have an instant house on your plot of land. It may not have sliding glass windows, but you will have a roof over your head and maybe stories to tell round the fire.

The Dip has its more lavish counterparts all over North America. Witness *The Cabin: Inspiration for the Classic American Getaway,* a book co-authored by Dale Mulfinger—an architect who writes a column called "Cabin Fever" for a Minneapolis magazine. The thirty-seven cabins captured in photos, drawings, and text are at times too glorious (all that honeyed wood aglow in sunlight), but I was also struck by how tiny and modest, how understated and ad hoc many of them were. None comprised more than twelve hundred square feet, and many were considerably smaller. Anything bigger was deemed to be a summer home, a cottage, or a lodge, and not, by definition, worthy of the name *cabin.*

One man built a twelve-by-eighteen-foot log cabin in Minnesota after taking a course in log construction and tackling the job on weekends over the course of a year. Working on land his grandparents had ceded him as a gift, he used timber from the property and cast-off windows, flooring, and roofing material—all of it restored or refinished with care. Much like our cabin, his has no running water and any showers taken are of the outdoor solar variety. The one-room cabin was built as a prototype for a larger one to follow. Total cost, building course included, for this startlingly elegant cabin: two thousand dollars. Often these tiny cabins become guest cabins, with novice builders learning from their mistakes (though perhaps making new ones) on the larger cabins that came later.

Another log cabin near Lake Superior, also humbly imagined, is only fourteen feet by sixteen feet, but its loft and porch make it feel bigger. It, too, calls to mind the Bresee/Scanlan cabin, with its varnished plywood countertops, ceramic water dispensers, the skirts round the lower cupboards, and the rain barrels outside. An old hewn log tobacco barn in the Blue Ridge Mountains of Virginia, originally built in the late 1800s, was rescued and has become a weekend getaway. "Sit Long. Talk Much. Laugh a Lot" reads a sign on the beam over the doorway. One cabin, a modern post-and-beam kit, was assembled on Puget Sound over the course of a three-week vacation. A Cape Cod garage was converted into a small cottage, with widow's walk, on a strict renovation budget of twenty thousand dollars.

An old aluminum trailer—think of those Airstream models from the 1950s—is somehow incorporated as a passageway and dining area in an artist's wildly eccentric cabin in the woods. Sailboat line is deployed as deck railing lest the view be spoiled. Inspired by fire lookouts in Montana, a glass-on-all-sides cabin is set on a high stone pedestal. A virtual glass house comes to occupy the Wisconsin prairie. A cabin overlooking Eel Bay, Nova

Scotia, is inspired by boat-building savvy; another cabin boasts a prow-shaped porch, and yet another cabin on Lake Superior bears the shape of an arc boldly facing the east and the rising sun.

There are cabins of wood, stone, corrugated tin, cement fibreboard, cabins fashioned from new logs, old logs, board and batten, a "folly" built to look like a silo, a cabin dubbed "Le Porch." Getaways with encircling porches, solar-powered cabins, minimalist shelters with homemade Murphy beds. The variety is both endless and inspiring.

What distinguishes many of these cabins is the way they blend into the landscape without ever trying to overpower. The view is the thing. Porches, decks, widows' walks—all draw the user outside, for walking in the meadow, for gathering wildflowers, for birdwatching or biking, for contemplating whatever warrants it. But so is simplicity the thing, and companionship and family. Many of the cabins in the book are one-room cabins, with lofts for sleeping accessed by ship's ladders. I saw lots of rocking chairs, bookshelves, and escritoires (but no televisions), hats on antlers and Monopoly games, and always, always, a woodstove or fireplace, candles and kerosene lamps, for a cabin must have fire. Almost all the cabins seem set apart—on lakes, by streams, in forests, on plains and mountains. I could almost hear the quiet.

The owner-built cabin in the great beyond is an old dream. *How to Build 20 Cabins,* for example, was published in New York in 1955. Unlike *The Cabin,* with its glossy colour and architectural landscape drawings, this little book features simple line drawings and overly dark black-and-white photographs of the various models. There is The Hermitage (designed to hug a hill), The Leisure House (an A-frame), The Six-Shooter (this was, and is,

America), The Scout (photo of man on porch checking his shotgun), The Hideout (Ma and Pa on the porch, both with hunting rifles), and The Seneca (hatted hunter, rifle in hand, bidding adieu to the missus at the screen door). The book's editor, Ray Gill, in his hand-signed foreword, expresses the hope that the reader finds "the one rustic refuge you've been dreaming about."

The cabin of our dreams is like the ones in these books. Unassailable and close to perfect. In such dreams, the work is done and was a breeze in any case, the sun is always shining, the roof wouldn't dream of leaking, and the bats, mice, and carpenter ants have no place here. Never did. As for the neighbour plotting to install a go-kart track at the property line or the gravel pit in the offing down the road, they have no place in this fantasy world either.

Perhaps because so much of my time is spent virtually still, sitting at a keyboard and waiting for the words to come, I am drawn to pure labour, and the less mentally taxing it is, the better. It's as if my body has been constrained in a box, and now it wants to move, to flex, to pick up the pace. So much work at the cabin fits that bill nicely.

All during the construction of the cabin, I would often end my day there cleaning up after the workers, sweeping up sawdust, hauling wood ends to the kindling pile, tidying boards piled in the tool shed. I was trying to impose a little order on the chaos. (As Michael sought to impose order on me, for there was a knack, he insisted, of laying the lumber down, with small crosspieces strategically placed to avoid warping.)

These days, cabin labour is painting floors and walls, cutting and splitting firewood, my odd (sometimes very odd) carpentry jobs that answer my body's need for repetitive motion. Cutting, hammering, sanding. The island counter in the kitchen, the bookcase by the entryway, the handyman's vanity in what I call the bathroom upstairs.

The Saskatchewan writer Sharon Butala talks about this in some of her books, how the difference between urban and rural folk is that the former tend to talk, while the latter simply do. So much anxiety in the city is played out in words, while in the country it drains away with hard toil.

Take splitting firewood, for example. Late one summer I was cutting up a hard maple that the wind had broken at the trunk, the strongest part of the tree. For every strong feature in nature (like a mature maple), there is one stronger (the west wind).

Splitting wood requires no thinking at all. It is the kind of work that Jack Kerouac—who called himself "an urban Thoreau"—would have wished on us all. Kerouac and his fellow beat generation writers were convinced that manual labour and time in the wilderness were the perfect antidotes to the consumerism they felt was poisoning North America in the 1960s. Kerouac manned a forest service lookout tower in the mountains, worked on a merchant marine ship, and served as a railroad brakeman. Nature and toil, he once said of the combination, "work the blood clots right out of existence."

I have split enough wood that I do it thoughtlessly, like skating and breathing and walking. Only when a sixteen-year-old boy from northern France named Olivier—a summer visitor to the cabin—sought instruction in the art of wood splitting did I stop to consider the mechanics. The maul is heavy, maybe twelve pounds, so as I raise the axe handle with both hands my left hand slides halfway down to aid in lifting. But when the handle reaches its apex in the air and stands vertical, that left hand slides back to join the right hand, in the style of a batter in baseball, and the maul comes down on the piece to be split. Said piece sits on another, more ample stump, which spares the axe digging into the ground. Ground, too, might otherwise give too much and forgive the blow.

It is amazing how some pieces split so readily and others so staunchly resist. Knots defy, as do certain woods such as oak and the aptly named ironwood. One trick is to give the maul a little sideways twist just before it meets the wood, so the force comes in, and down, at a little angle. It helps to envision, as athletes do before games, the desired outcome before it occurs.

After an hour or so, the sweat flowing freely from my brow, there is dry bark at my feet and a smell in the air—almost sweet—of resins and time, seasons and sap. Even the old pine boards rescued as flooring for the cabin release that woody perfume when cut.

The hat I sometimes wear in the sun is my grandfather's, its usual home a nail set into the centre beam at the cabin. I dearly wish he could have seen this place, but Leonard Flynn died in 1982, six years before we bought the land. At least he saw our place in Camden East and got to laugh at our mistakes (like the vocal rooster who nearly drove me mad and ended up in Grandpa's chicken pot pie).

I have the old colourized aerial photo of the farm that hung at their place on Markland Street in Kingston. I have his cane—a plain oak model with rubber tip, a cane I plan to use myself one day if I live long enough ("if I'm spared," as some say). And I have one of my grandfather's sweat-stained fedoras, a Biltmore SNAP-amatic (*Patent Pending), grey felt with matching grey band and a jaunty red and blue feather that remains fresh and new by forever hiding from view and ducking behind the band. This is my wood-splitting hat, and I think of its original owner every time I pick up the maul. I think of all the wood he would have cut by hand, for their woodstoves were not airtight and went through fuel like a whale through plankton. He would have used a cross-cut saw, maybe working with a friend or neighbour, someone likely named Murphy or O'Connor or Way. Maybe he wore the grey SNAP-amatic. Funny and wise, mischievous and kind, a teller of tales, an occasional cheater at euchre, my grandfather was grateful for all he had. Which was not a lot. A rock farm near Tamworth, Ontario. A hard life. Barely a chamber pot to pee in. (It was reserved for illness, severe winter weather, or emergencies; otherwise the privy down by the orchard did the job.)

Leonard Flynn had that farmer's optimism that next year would be better, that the rains would come or hold off, as need be. He was grateful for the old age security cheque that came in the mail; astonished, more like it. He couldn't quite fathom being paid for being old. A lifetime of scrabbling will do that. I may be wrong about this, but I do believe there are salvation and redemption, even joy, in hard toil. It is perhaps why the dispossessed of the world laugh more easily than we do in the mostly affluent West. They ask for little, and get less. We ask for more and cannot be sated.

That's why my simple projects around the cabin, in the surrounding fields and forest, feel so right to me.

"Do you never get lonely at the cabin?" David asked me one day. When he taught high school, he would spend several weeks at a time on his land during the summer, bunking with the mice in the trailer, cutting grass and tending Hutch's vines in the morning and penning his novel in the afternoon. Then he would scurry home to Toronto, reconnect with family and friends, and return refreshed and ready once more for the hermitage. Along the way he acquired the writer's discipline, and it has paid off, but he never warmed to long stretches of solitude. He'd find himself of an evening at a sports bar in town chatting up the barflies while watching a Jays game or lining up a date to play pool with a musician friend. The days alone left him longing for human prattle.

I know the feeling, but I embrace my solitary bouts more wholeheartedly than my friend does. It's not that I love humans less; it's the spectator in me that finds its fullest satisfaction in being alone and watchful outdoors. When I was a boy, growing up in the 1950s in the then young suburb of Scarborough, I would bike—with friends or alone—to what seemed a vast park. Wexford Park it was called, after County Wexford in Ireland. We used its several ball diamonds and open fields for baseball and touch football, but it was the ten-acre woods that held me most in thrall. (Later, as a university student, I would pass several blissful summers as sole warden of the park, paid by the municipality to cut the grass, keep the park clean, and mark out the diamonds before ball games.) Boys of ten or twelve, we would take lunches and spend entire days in and around the tall forest, looking for snakes and frogs to maim and destroy. I am appalled to recall what we did. The worst was putting firecrackers in the mouths of frogs, lighting the wick, and delighting in the blast. We would take magnifying glasses and fry ants; cripple a black ant and deposit it at the nest of its enemy, the red ant, and watch it being drawn down into the hole as so much live food; we would offer innocent worms to the hordes, which attacked along the poor thing's length. Little Neros and their savage little circuses. We were no better, and, in some ways, worse, than nineteenth-century buffalo hunters who shot from trains or the casual sharpshooters of the nineteenth century who practised their marksmanship on passenger pigeons. Today, I wouldn't hurt a fly (cluster flies excepted), though I still marvel at the same things that entranced me as a boy. When I wasn't frying ants, I was reading about them and admiring them—their extraordinary strength, their determination, their ferocity, their ingenuity. I would spend hours watching one colony or individuals under a microscope.

One day at the cabin, I happened to see an animated line of fierce black-red ants going to and from the heavy stone that serves as a step at the cabin's south door. The ones departing were carrying small eggs, smaller than rice kernels. It was high summer and Ulrike was there, along with Kurt and a friend from France, Pierre-Édouard. That morning, we lifted the rock, set it on its side, and observed the carnage. Hundreds of skirmishes were under way, the black ants trying desperately to defend the nest and their young, the black-red raiders intent on thieving eggs and slaying any defenders in their way. There is no etiquette in human warfare, and surely none in the order Hymenoptera. Two ants would savage one. Severed heads fought other severed heads. Striking with claw and stinger, ants grappled and circled like sumo wrestlers, and while the battle ensued, so did the marauding and plundering of hundreds of prized white eggs—future slaves for the raiders' own colony. All day it went on, long after we spectators had had our fill of the silent drama. Only at sunset, when we set the rock back in place, had combat ceased. But you knew that if the black colony survived, the black-reds would come again.

Jean-Henri Fabre, the French entomologist who died in 1915, was called the insects' Homer. In his ten-volume *Souvenirs entomologiques,* he describes how a bee-eating wasp will squeeze the crop of the honey-laden bee "so as to make her disgorge the delicious syrup, which she drinks by licking the tongue which her unfortunate victim, in her death-agony, sticks out of her mouth at full length … At the moment of some such horrible banquet, I have seen the Wasp, with her prey, seized by the Mantis: the bandit was rifled by another bandit. And here is an awful detail: while the Mantis held her transfixed under the points of the double saw and was already munching her belly, the Wasp continued to lick the honey of her Bee, unable to relinquish the delicious food even amid the terrors of death."

In 1856, Henry David Thoreau described catching a pickerel that had just swallowed three perch, one of which was taken at the very moment it was swallowing a minnow.

Annie Dillard, who writes like an angel, does not flinch at the ghoulish business unfolding on the soil, in the grasses, the lakes and rivers. She is a writer I admire deeply, not least for the sense of wonder she brings to all nature, and especially insects, and her longing to know the divine. In *Pilgrim at Tinker Creek,* she does not ask why a reasonable god would allow earth's creatures to inflict such cruelty on each other. Dillard both accepts, and delights in, the carnivorous chain (and one can imagine the bee-wasp-mantis link extending, the mantis set upon by a bird, the bird by a snake, the snake by a hawk ...). Such acts, she says, are "mysteries performed in broad daylight before our very eyes" and since there are infinitely more insects than there are humans, "theirs is the biggest wedge of the pie ... I look to them for a glimmer of companionship."

The cabin, without and within, seems to foster both watchfulness and a delight in small beauties—though perhaps they are not small at all. I think of that open room on the cabin's main floor, how the sunlight casts window-shaped patterns on the terra cotta–painted floor, on the table where we dine, on the hearth's south face.

On rare occasions, I've had to leave the cabin on a winter's evening and pack up in the dark. When the doors are all locked, I cannot resist the temptation to look inside as a voyeur might. The woodstove will flash and send light arcing across the room, dancing on the floor and against the couch in front of the fire, as if some old movie were playing in there. How melancholy is an unwatched fire; I feel a great compulsion to witness the flames at least till they're blood-red embers. It's always hard to leave the cabin, but this kind of leave-taking is the worst.

I feel shut out and almost jealous of that florid couch—plucked from Ulrike's office and brilliant in the firelight. The couch pattern is rose and white, and busy, a pattern my grandmothers might have chosen for a party dress. I was determined to cover the couch when I first hauled it in and placed it before the hearth, convinced it was wildly out of place amid the plain greys and heritage browns. But I grew to love the infusion of colour it brought to the room, and I liked the way those roses caught the fire of the western sun and the roiling maple behind the glass of the woodstove. Even the terra cotta paint we had chosen to dress up the plywood floor seemed to find a mate amid the florid patterns of that couch.

Goethe possessed an astonishing range of interests beyond drama and literature—the law, human anatomy, botany, geology. He once wrote, "To live within limits, to want one thing, or a very few things, very much and love them dearly, cling to them, survey them from every angle, become one with them—that is what makes the poet, the artist, the human being." Substitute *a piece of land* for *one thing* or *a very few things* and you have what made the life and times of Goethe's contemporary, Henry David Thoreau, so special. He dearly loved that patch of land at Walden Pond, and did indeed cling to it, survey it from every angle, and become one with it.

It wasn't actually his—friend and fellow writer, Ralph Waldo Emerson, had bought the fifteen-acre tract on the north shore of the pond in 1844—but Thoreau had been coming to the pond since he was four years old. For years, the thought of building a cabin on the pond and living there had been a dream. When he acquired building skills and his friend acquired the land, the dream got hammered into being.

In *Henry David Thoreau: A Life of the Mind*, Robert D. Richardson Jr. points out that Thoreau was said to be of ordinary stature—bulbous nose, medium height, fine light brown hair. What set him apart were his eyes—"strong, serious, large, and deep set; bright blue in some lights, gray in others. As he walked around Concord people noticed that his eyes rarely left the ground. When he did look up, however, he swept in everything at a glance. His eyes had a startling earnestness, and they were alight with intelligence and humor."

Thoreau was as much walker as writer. And he noticed everything on those walks—keeping voluminous notes on what he saw and heard and felt. (He complained of not being able to buy blank notebooks to record his thoughts and that the only notepads available in Concord were ledgers ruled for accounting.) He walked vigorously and far, hours at a time. Visiting Walden Pond and working in his garden there in 1837, he felt a pure contentment and a connection with nature. The Maryland yellowthroat, he was convinced, was singing "Ecstasy, ecstasy." Thoreau spent just twenty-six months actually living at Walden Pond, but they would be the most productive months of his writing life. He was extraordinarily, intensely alive and attuned to that woods, that pond.

His sense of the divine found expression there. God was so literally in those trees that, when Thoreau was dying in 1862, he wrote that autumn leaves "teach us how to die." And when an aunt asked him on his deathbed if he had made his peace with God, he replied, famously, "I did not know we had ever quarrelled."

One of the last books Thoreau read was *What Can Be Learned from a Tree,* and he took sustenance from the fact that a barren field could become a vital forest in only fifteen years' time. Two years before his death, he expressed the desire to be buried in such a forest, in "a soil thus wide-awake."

I had always seen Thoreau as a naturalist and as a writer, but Richardson's book is very much about the man as scholar. Thoreau read widely and voraciously. He once copied out a lost passage from Aristotle that perhaps captured his own sense of nature's godliness. Aristotle was postulating that if otherwise fortunate beings from some distant place "should suddenly behold the earth, and the sea, and the vault of heaven; should perceive the broad expanse of the clouds, and the strength of the winds, should admire the sun in his majesty, beauty and effulgence, and lastly when night veiled the earth in darkness, should gaze on the starry firmament, the waxing and waning moon and the stars rising and setting in the unchanging course ordained from eternity, they would, of a truth, exclaim 'there are gods, and such great things are their work.'"

Near the end of his life, Thoreau moved toward a middle position, arguing that the ideal life gathered from both the civilized and the savage, from the refined and the wild. Thoreau saw himself living a "border life," spending time in nature for nourishment but knowing full well that he couldn't live there permanently. He had, as many others have since, a foot in both camps. And whatever chord Thoreau struck, it still resonates. E.B. White remarked in 1954—almost a century after Thoreau's death—that "*Walden Pond* is not the best book I ever encountered, perhaps, but is for me the handiest, and I keep it about me in much the same way one carries a handkerchief—for relief in moments of fluxion or despair."

water

When my family and I traded our house in a village for one in a city in the spring of 1998, we gained in some ways. Queen's University, where Ulrike would earn a teaching degree that fall, was literally down the street and no longer nineteen miles away. Kurt's high school—the oldest in Canada and said to be the best one in Kingston—was a five-minute walk away, as were fine libraries, cinemas, and restaurants. It felt good to walk or cycle and not always have to drive.

And I like our city house. I even like the *convenience*—a word I would hear repeatedly as the hallmark of city life. Many people had been fed the same pablum: city life = convenience, and its corollary, country life = inconvenience. Trouble was, and is, I *loved* our village house and still mourn it. My book *Heading Home* was about country life, pros and cons, but much of my script was written in praise of our grand old clapboard house built in 1867, the one that graced the book's cover. The night we took possession of the city house, we made a trip to town, got the keys, and went inside our new home. The intention was to take supplemental measurements since some hefty country furniture—the harvest table, my bookcases—was now destined for slimmer urban digs. The new place was a little sad, as all empty houses are, and Uly was going about her business, moving from tape measure to note pad, methodically writing down numbers, laying out rooms, assigning our tables and couches and chairs to their allotted places. Until she turned to teaching, Uly was a designer—of books and magazines—and layout is still her domain.

Kurt and I, meanwhile, walked about ceremoniously, trying to get the feel of the place, our steps and voices echoing as we went. We were like dogs sniffing at trees and posts in a new park. Then all business ceased, Ulrike sat down heavily by the beautifully wide and ample window well we would later fill with plants, and the tears came. That some furnishings weren't going to fit was only part of the problem; it was that other fit, of human and house. The old one had been so right, and this one was plagued with uncertainty. I tried to console her, assured her that this was a splendid house, that we would be happy here. Kurt did the same, but he actually believed his own words. Mine lacked conviction. In my heart I grieved as much as Ulrike did.

Five years later, Ulrike seems more at home in the city, more comfortable with the choice we made. She has stamped the backyard with her own touch, rounded and recast the perennial gardens. Kurt settled quickly into his new abode and, after initially choosing a second-floor bedroom, wisely claimed the third-floor loft—briefly the guest room—as his own. Even Dusty adjusted better than I did (though the park close by couldn't hold a candle to the old railway line we used to walk). I'm the one who failed to put down roots. Our midtown house is where I live, and happily enough, but the cabin is where I now breathe most deeply.

The cabin has taken the place of our house on Mill Street in the village, and the passage of time has helped me understand why the latter loomed so large. In leaving it, we forfeited the intimacy of the village circle and a sense of neighbourhood that extended for miles. The seasonal round was engraved on us out there, and countless rituals marked their passing: planting seeds in the spring, cutting and splitting wood in the summer, the fall harvest, Christmas carols at the little barn by the river. We left behind cleaner air, starry skies, and northern lights, that dead quiet that would fall over the village at night—and the river.

I had slung a hammock between two Manitoba maples at the top of the bank, and it gave me great pleasure to lie in the hammock's ropey embrace and listen to the river's gurgle. Every rush, every eddy up and down that river—sleepy in August, muscular in spring, alluring and white in winter—calmed me. Kurt and I fished there (a photo shows him at two, rod in hand and sitting all business in the shallows on a blue cloth fold-up camp chair), we all three of us canoed there, on hot days I'd dunk my feet in that river. For the ducks we raised, the river was home and they would range far up- and downriver, always coming when I called them for a feed of grain. The water would carry my whistle—seven long straight blows, always seven—and it might be several minutes before I saw the flotilla steaming upstream, loudly quacking. I loved that river, even the damp ripe smells that emanated from the banks at night spring through fall, and its loss made a great hole at my centre.

For seventeen years, we lived in that village on that river, and I still miss the tinkle of ice in winter and the swollen surge in spring (the river's reply to any who dared call it a creek). It became a ritual of spring to open the north-facing sliding glass doors to let in that rush of sound. And it was there, the Napanee River, right there. So many nights I would go out and lean my elbows on the deck we had built at the high bank, just to hear it. There was something soothing about that ritual.

That first summer in the city I bought a small fountain, the desktop kind sometimes seen in offices. A small electric pump drives water up through ersatz rock and the water tumbles down a fake cliff and drops into a rock-filled pool below, whereupon the circle is repeated. I was trying to mask the sound of traffic on our street. In the village, cars passed in front of our house about twice a day; in the city it was twice a minute.

Then I dug a hole in the backyard and installed a black plastic pond the size of an ample bathtub, filled it with water, and plugged in another pump, one that powered a fountain's circular spray in the middle. I would sit there at the round picnic table, nurse my pipe, and look west at the end of the day over the splendid garden that Ulrike had fashioned back there. Only later did it occur to me that both fountains were my feeble attempt to retrieve the river.

I had gotten used to the company of water, and I am not alone. Water has become fashionable as a garden element. Many people I know have backyard ponds, filled bathtubs with goldfish and established water gardens. Another friend with a swimming pool had the builders install something similar to my office fountain, only ten times the size. The sound of water dropping from a height is as good as a massage.

It seems we are remembering what our ancestors knew. Edith Wharton, the American novelist, wrote a book in 1904, *Italian*

Villas and Their Gardens, in which she noted that Italian gardens of the Renaissance and baroque periods were alive with "rushing or motionless water." Lavish villas featured an endless array of fountains, streams, reflecting pools, and water jets. In one villa, a vigorous mountain stream flowed right through a central apartment. Here is Wharton describing the Villa d'Este at Tivo, near Rome:

"From the Anio, drawn up the hillside at incalculable cost and labour, a thousand rills gush downward, terrace by terrace, channelling the stone rails of the balusters, leaping from step to step, dripping into mossy conchs, flashing in spray from the horns of sea-gods and the jaws of mythical monsters." Wharton called the gardens "an organ on which the water played."

She noted that these elaborate gardens were designed to be *lived in;* and the test of that truth is that the nobility of the day made their villas small and simple, preferring to devote their time and wealth to their gardens. The privileged of the sixteenth century sought to marry art and nature, house and hillside, villa and view. Harmony of line, balance between sun and shadow, the blue of the sky caught in reflecting pools, "the garden-magic" that springs from marble, water, and verdant glory: all this mattered to landscape architects of the day. They and their clients were forever looking out.

Wharton's book has been embellished by Maxwell Parrish illustrations, one of them showing a monk lost in his book and walking the gardens at The Cascade, Villa Torlonia, at Frascati. You can see the hillside where the water falls from one stone basin to the next, four in all and each one a little wider than the one above. You can almost hear the sound of falling water, feel its pull, the gentle spray drifting on the wind. The monk is not real, just lines on a page, yet I envy him nonetheless, his surroundings, his companionable cascade.

Maybe you've seen pictures of the Frank Lloyd Wright house near Connellsville, Pennsylvania. Built in 1936 as a rich man's cottage, the stone and concrete structure was cantilevered over a waterfall and ravine called Bear Run, with a suspended staircase allowing the user to sit on steps just above the tumbling water. Wright called his creation Fallingwater and his biographer, Meryle Secrest, calls its creation "one of the most famous moments in architecture … tantamount to being at Mozart's elbow the day he dipped his quill pen and began to compose *The Magic Flute*." I'm not sure about tantamount, but it is a good tale. (One dashed by a new book on Wright, which argues that Fallingwater was not born of a moment's inspiration but of a life's work.)

Wright had visited Bear Run several times and had told his client—a department store magnate named Edgar J. Kaufmann—that the design was finished (it had not, in fact, even been started). With the client en route to Wright's study that morning, the great man sat in his bathrobe at a table near the fire in his study/bedroom and began to draw. Two feverish hours and many pencils later, it was done. Wright was sixty-eight years old and he had created a masterpiece that melded earth, wind, fire, and water. It had seemed to Wright "the natural thing" to build a house—not where the client had suggested, looking up at the cascade from below—but on that high ledge of rock, a house as a series of interlapping concrete trays set one atop the other, a house without walls but with spectacular glass vistas, a house not with a view of the falls but *of* the falls.

The pond I dream of would lack both the opulence and imagination of Fallingwater, but it would be as big as the underground source—and my budget—would allow; most certainly, the pond I imagine would feature that sound of water cascading. The road that fronts part of our parcel of land is quiet; a vehicle passes every hour or so in summer and traffic falls off almost completely in other seasons or after dark. My dream pond and its little falls would shut out even the road's bit of manufactured noise.

My pond would form in the middle field behind the cabin. My own Walden. Big enough and deep enough for a little punt or rowboat; a home for our old river canoe, now wedged forlornly between cedars. A pond for fish and frogs, for herons and ducks, for deer and foxes and coyotes, and any two-legged philosophers who would agree with Lao-tzu, a Chinese sage who was arguing almost three-thousand years ago that "The wise man delights in water."

Early in August of 2002, water took Michael Keeling, the gifted carpenter who had guided the cabin into being. After 1997, I would see him occasionally—the old *Harrowsmith* gang used to meet once a month in Kingston for drinks at the Grizzly Grill (with its square-timbered cabin motif), and he'd be there with his wife, Mirielle. He would always want to know about the cabin: What changes had I made? When was I last there? And, especially, did I still love it? When his part in the cabin's restoration was done, he had taken several trips—Mirielle in tow on one occasion, his mother, Marie, on another—so that he and some of those he loved could admire the cabin. He was as proud of the place as I was, and sometimes at those monthly reunions he would press me on some detail, urge me to add a fascia board on the tool shed or some trim on the second floor of the cabin.

But on August 3, 2002, he perished in a freak accident. Just weeks after his fifty-first birthday, he was moving his canoe on the Salmon River behind the splendid house he had largely built himself on a back road near Tamworth. Perhaps, the police would later speculate, he stood in the canoe to catch a better view of an otter or a beaver, lost his balance, struck his head on the gunwale, and fell into the water. I was among those asked to speak at Michael's funeral, and this, in part, is what I said:

For Michael
August 7, 2002
Tamworth, Ontario

I spent the better part of 1996 and into '97 as a carpenter's apprentice, though apprentice *sounds too glorious: carpenter's helper, go-fer, goof is more like it. There was no doubting my lack of skill, no doubting the skill of the carpenter, for the real builder on the work site those years was Michael Richard Keeling. A reed of a man in a wide-brimmed hat, a carpenter's apron at his waist, hands on hips as he faced down yet another carpenter conundrum. And on this job there were many such conundrums.*

Every morning he would come by early, park his rusting old Ford truck at our place in Camden East, and we'd drive for ninety minutes to what I called "the land." During those long hours on the road with him, at the site with him all day, on the telephone with him almost every evening, the cabin rising by fits and starts, log by log … my education, my real *education, began. I had tried to teach Michael what I knew about craft: mine was the Red Green school of duct tape and chicken wire. Michael's sorry task was to set me straight.*

I'm going to the cabin later on today for a few nights, Ulrike is hosting friends there on Friday night, and our son, Kurt, and a friend are coming on the weekend. It will not be the usual time at the cabin. We'll all be thinking of Michael, for his stamp is all over that place.

Michael learned his trade by taking building courses at Algonquin College; but he also studied at the feet of some rough-hewn tradesmen. He and I would be hammering nails alongside one another, up on the tool shed roof, say, and he'd remember what one of the old gaffers used to tell him as he *nailed. "Good enough for the girls we run with," the old fellow would say. It sounds so light-hearted, so casual, the words of someone willing to cut corners. But Michael was very, very serious about his craft; he did not cut corners. He would tilt me in the direction of the best choice in wood, the priciest nails and hardware, quality windows. Michael Keeling* loved *quality.*

He wore his work as some men wear aftershave. He smelled of sawdust and every wood he worked with—pine and oak and cherry, maple and birch and ash. He smelled of toil and leather and nails. He had great sympathy for other workmen on the job—the roofer, the mason, the electrician, the backhoe operator—and sometimes he would act as peacemaker when I wanted to strangle some of them for not showing up or for shoddy workmanship. He loathed shoddy workmanship and could be severely critical; but when someone else's work was spot on, he was full of praise. Indeed, such excellence cheered him. Michael Keeling loved beauty and embraced it wherever he saw it. His diploma, you should know, was in photography. His passions ranged from music to baking. Asked to describe him, in a word, a friend said solid, *then she added, "I never saw him in a shirt and tie. Did you?" I never did.*

Michael loved old values: symmetry, strength, simplicity. His tool box declared him: It was not the modern metal kind but the old wooden model, the grandfather type—open, with a long dowling handle.

He was not religious in the usual sense, but anyone who treasures trees, as he did (he was obsessed with them), surely has a sense of the sacred, a sense of the divine. Michael especially loved oaks and nut trees, and he planted them by the hundreds all over the sanctuary he and Mirielle built not far from here. Mirielle tells me that Michael was always a spiritual person, and becoming more so; to be out in his canoe on the Salmon River at dawn—with the otters and beavers and herons—was, for him, a kind of ceremony, a moment of kinship.

Whatever his theology, Michael certainly knew about sin. Sin was leaving a tool out in the rain. I did that once, left his utility knife in the grass. He let it be known that that yellow cutter—and the germ of rust that he was sure had infiltrated the tool's steel heart—was now mine; he expected, and got, a new one. (I still have his, by the way, in my tool box.)

He abhorred noise, valued quiet, and spoke softly, always. He loved animals (though he could be hard on chewing rodents, such as the mice and beavers that girdled his precious trees), he loved birds and flowers and nature, he loved the very river that took him. And he loved Mirielle—her brightness, her laughter and irreverence, her silly side—and my guess is that she kept him level, plumb, and square, as all carpenters should be. For a man who seemed so shy and private, he was remarkably forceful and regular, almost daily, in his declarations of love—to his mother, Marie, to Mirielle. For him, it was a kind of salutation, as if he knew that every day might be the last one and that every declaration was, just maybe, the final one.

"I miss him already," Mirielle told me last night. I will miss the pairing of them, the rare good fit of friend and lover. MK and MK. Who can think of Mirielle without thinking of Michael? But in the bracing cool breezes that swirled round their house two nights ago, Mirielle said she could feel Michael's spirit. "It'll be OK," the spirit said to her. "It'll be OK."

Many of us in this room count Michael-built things among our possessions. A house, a cabin, a garage, a bookshelf, a chair. Go home, run your hands over the wood he worked on, try to feel the grain, admire the design, the care and craft that went into it. This isn't Michael's only legacy, but it's the one I feel closest to, and this fall, when a chill descends on the cabin, I'll fire up the Regency woodstove—the one with the glass door we bought from Michael and Mirielle—I'll stare into the flames and remember the man, his gifts, his quiet enduring legacy. The memories we have of him, all that he built, and trees. Trees and trees and trees.

My plan is to buy a seedling and plant it on the south side of the cabin so that long after I've gone, the spreading limbs of the Keeling oak will keep the cabin cool and lend the land a little grace. I think he'd like that.

[As a postscript, you should know that in the fall Mirielle invited many of her friends to take home as many of Michael's seedlings as we cared to. I took to the cabin more than a dozen—edible pine, spice bush, pagoda dogwood, white oak, bear oak, and several little ones we could not name but will plant in memory of the man who nurtured them into being.]

Seven weeks after the death by drowning of Michael Keeling, Ulrike and I went to his place near Tamworth for a gathering of friends. Mirielle took me into a screened room at the back of the house where at sunset, in the late evening, and every morning she looks upon Michael's pond. I was filled with wonder that something so simple could weave such magic.

I tried to imagine the thing in its infancy. A six-foot-square concrete box, the cement six inches thick, the box four feet deep. Early on it must have looked like a sepulchre. But the night

I gazed upon it, I was transfixed. Fat frogs, frogs the size of softballs, lounged in the water by lily pads or camped out on the margins. Smug frog princes. Mirielle had strung tiny white lights around a bush at the perimeter so that from the screened-in room, the pond was the very centre of that little speck of the universe. The only other lights you could see were stars.

"We used to feed the frogs tomato worms," Mirielle told us, laughing as she did, "but the frogs got so huge we stopped." Call it Weight Watchers for amphibians. But whatever the frogs were dining on these days, they remained well fed. No doubt the tiny white lights also drew small insects, moths, and June bugs—room service for bull frogs. They glistened, as Jabba the Hut glistened.

In that screened room was a table flanked by two chairs. Every morning Mirielle would sit there and look west toward the pond, the house behind acting as a buffer against the morning sun and the searing heat that the summer of '02 inflicted. The pond would have reflected the muted morning light. At sunset, the pond would have refracted the light of the still bold sun. And at night, the white lights skirting the bush would have mimicked the stars above. I thought, all this joy from a little box of water. I would have such a box, such a pond.

I left the party inside to crouch by the pond, squatted down by the frogs, listened to the crickets, took in the darkness and the moon and felt the kind of peace I never feel in my own backyard in the city.

Driving home that night, the road south pocked with the bodies of squashed and yet to be squashed frogs (how were they to know that perching on that warm black flatness would be their last act?), I thought of the pond I would make. *Pace* Michael.

I thought of the frogs I would borrow from these same roads on rainy nights and of the music these rescued frogs would make in the fields around and about the cabin.

In their classic book, the authors of *A Pattern Language* outline some of the guiding principles behind houses that work. One of the ideals the authors cite is proximity to water—not a swimming pool whose dropoff would menace young children, but a natural pool with a shoreline that gradually deepens, a pool where children can wade, toss sticks, and skip stones, where a man or a woman can lie still and see what creatures come.

The cabin, or at least my being there, is suffused in ritual, one of them the five-minute drive to the Point on sunny summer days to swim and watch the play of light on water and the sun descend. "We're going to the Point," I will announce to Dusty and she always responds gleefully. She will rear like a playful colt, walk toward me on two legs, then land at my feet and dive into a crouch, circle happily and rear again. *The Point* is, for her, a cherished phrase in her vocabulary, right up there with *walk* and *treat* and *bunny*.

The coastline at the Point is ragged limestone that wind and water have carved into so many chipped and U-shaped bays, some so small and deep that they virtually encase the sitter, like a child in the clasp of her grandmother; some are wide with lofty perches, and everywhere great shelves of limestone slide into the water.

In eons past, that stone was under water. Four hundred million years ago—during what paleontologists call the Ordovician period of the Paleozoic era—the limestone I love to perch on lay at the bottom of a warm and shallow inland sea. Over the course of two hundred million years, silt and coral and the bodies of dead sea creatures drifted slowly to the bottom and the great weight of water above compacted and hardened them. Then, one million years ago, came the glaciers—advancing and retreating repeatedly, leaving sand and gravel and silt behind each time. Grasses would follow, then trees.

When the ice finally receded for what seemed the last time, the mastodons, mammoths, and caribou took heed of the global warming and occupied county lands. Their presence drew Paleo-Indians, hunters whose spear points attest to their presence in this area ten thousand years before the birth of Christ. So-called mound builders would follow, and leave behind pottery, pipes, and, for their selected dead, elaborate pits with mounds overtop. By AD 1550, early Algonquin tribes were in the county, but they would eventually move northwest to form the Huron Confederacy while the Iroquois occupied the land south of Lake Ontario. For a long time, the county served as a neutral zone, a no-man's land between the two confederacies.

The county, a virtual island and small at that, had proven too luscious a target for war parties paddling by and offered too narrow a range for hunters of game. The first white person to set foot on the county may have been Samuel de Champlain, who likely spent a night on these shores in the fall of 1615 as he paddled with some five hundred Indians and fourteen fellow French toward upper New York State and a raid on the Iroquois. He liked what he saw: "It was a rich and cheery county. Along the shores one would think trees had been planted in most places," and he remarked on the vines, the walnut trees, the plenitude of fish. But "this lovely region" was uninhabited, he wrote, "for its Indian population had abandoned it in fear of Iroquois raiders."

Eventually, an Iroquois tribe, the Cayugas, would migrate to the county in pursuit of the beaver, whose fur they traded for axes and copper, blankets and beads offered by Europeans. For twelve hard years here, 1668 to 1680, a fairly new order of priests, the Order of St. Sulpice, tried for their share of Jesuit glory, saving the souls of savages while avoiding starvation themselves. But when the game and beaver gave out, the black robes gave up and their Kenté (or Quinte) mission on the west side of the county closed forever.

In the eighteenth century, the county would serve as a kind of refuge—for Indians and whites alike. A peaceful tribe of Iroquois, the Mississauga, would shelter in the county, as would United Empire Loyalists fleeing the United States after that country's war of independence.

Within a generation of that war, as if a shot had been fired to start a race, the entire county (all 250,000 acres) was surveyed and settled. But the notion of the county as a place of refuge for people seeking privacy and fleeing war seems to have endured. Sir John A. Macdonald professed to love the county. "They vote for me time after time," he reportedly said, "and they never ask me for anything. And they never get anything."

This, in capsule, is the pre-history and history of the virtual island wherein the cabin sits.

It's crown land all around the Point and few but locals know it exists, so time at the Point is often as private as it is contemplative. I imagine that all over Prince Edward County men and women and children have struck up their own relationships with nearby points of land: Grassy Point, Green Point, Grenade Point, Massasauga Point, Miller Point, Peats Point, Petticoat Point, Pierson Point, Pleasant Point, Point Petre, Potter Point, Robison Point, Salmon Point, Point Traverse—to name only a few.

As much as I love to watch the water, and especially late in the day when the light shimmers, I sometimes spend hours at the Point with my eyes closed so that I can focus on the surf as it breaks and rolls from left to right. No sound system in the world, no symphony, can match the sound of those rollers.

The Point has more voices than my river ever did. The river was a short story; the lake is an epic novel. For some reason, Lake Ontario is the Rodney Dangerfield of lakes; it gets no respect. Until quite recently, "cottage country" for Torontonians always meant going north, northwest, northeast. Those of us who lived there turned our backs on the lake the Indians called Ontario—"beautiful lake" or "sparkling water."

Lake Ontario is truly a great lake, 7,334 square miles in size, and small only in comparison to the greatest great lake, Superior, at 32,810 square miles. Superior is deeper, too: 1,332 feet compared to Ontario's 774 feet. But when I sit at the Point and look west, as I often do at sunset, my vantage is one hundred and eighty degrees, and there seems to be no end of sky or water. It's as if the great inland sea the geologists called Lake Iroquois had never morphed, for the sea is what I think of when I pay my homage to the sun.

Testament, too, to the girth of these waters is that the Great Lakes have swallowed hundreds of ships. At the tourist office in town, you can buy a map called "Wrecks of Eastern Lake Ontario and the Upper St. Lawrence," which proclaims this area "the best fresh water wreck diving in the world." And so I know that when I sit at the Point and gaze west at the setting sun, I am also staring at a watery graveyard, with sixteen sites marked and many more yet to be discovered. I sometimes wonder whether that fact adds to the appeal of the place. All my life I have been drawn to graveyards, their quiet dignity, the hints of lives past that granite markers convey.

I remember a graveyard high on a hill overlooking Woody Point on the west coast of Newfoundland; to walk that cemetery and read the stones was to be briefed on the often callous history of all outports. The children who fell through ice or were taken by smallpox; the women who died in childbirth; the men lost at sea or on the ice floes. I remember graveyards in Ireland, where the dead are buried in front of the church, not behind, and the faithful must face all those Celtic crosses—and their own mortality—on the way to mass. I thought it macabre at first; now it seems to make sense.

There are no markers at the Point, though its dead are many. The steamer *Commodore Barry* sank off the Point in 1842. *Jessie,* a schooner, in 1870. The schooners *Lady Moulton* and *International,* 1880. *Julia,* 1887. The schooner *Persia,* 1894.

The tale of the *Jessie,* in particular, is a wrenching one. Newspaper stories and township histories offer a grim account of the 126-foot-long schooner laden with fifteen thousand bushels of wheat "going to pieces" on Halloween night in a "fearful gale" off Salmon Point, with all nine hands lost. A man who tended the lighthouse there, Amos MacDonald, observed that in all his years he had never seen such a gale. The *Jessie,* he said, "was so close in we could have talked to the crew had it not been for the roaring wind." Four men and a woman were clinging to the main boom, waving and beseeching the farmers and fishermen onshore to help them, but "pyramids of water" came between them. The wind, Amos recalled, "piled up seas like houses."

Amos remembers all too well what happened next. "I can see him yet," he said, "as in a nightmare. One young, tall and powerful man decided to swim to shore. He was so close I could see the colour of his hair. He was a strong swimmer, and he struck out parallel to the beach so as to take the best chance with the undertow. Hundreds were watching him, encouraging him. Twice he came so close he could stand up on the bar with the seas only as high as his waist. Twice he was swept out again by the undertow before those on shore could grasp him. He was a long time fighting for his life." Did no one, I wondered as I read that awful account, have a rope to toss him? What must it have been like to be on that shore and to look on as a man, by degrees, drowned?

The surf, it appears, was thick with timbers and planks from the wreckage, and when a piece of the schooner's railing cuffed him on the head, the sailor disappeared below the waves. They found only one body afterwards, and someone took note of the ring on the third finger of his right hand—a large silver ring, with a raised anchor on top. A county point had claimed another victim.

The twentieth century also had its losses, with October and November proving the cruelest months. The *Owen* went down on

October 12, 1902. The *Charles Horn,* a steam barge, in 1910. The tug *Frank Barnes,* on November 10, 1915. The *Derbyshire,* a steamer, sank east of the Point on October 11, 1924. The most recent wreck listed is the *Empire,* a sidewheeler that also sank east of the Point in 1970.

Even tidal waves are not unknown on the county's several points. One hit Wicked Point in 1963 and took five minutes to pass over, leaving three feet of water on the land. One fishing boat weighing six tons was lifted by the wave and parked neatly in a large tree. There are 209 shipwrecks in all listed on the map of wrecks, and it strikes me that some of the ships' names did seem to tempt a dire fate: *Waterwitch, Banshee, Titanic.* Fire was the undoing of some lost ships, but most simply succumbed to the wrath of the lake.

During Prohibition in the 1920s and early 1930s, the south shore of the county was used as a staging ground for boats dashing across the lake with contraband liquor. These were dangerous runs, and the rum-runners were as likely to be sprayed with gunfire by vagabond smugglers as by the Coast Guard. The waters off the Point, then, are a graveyard for both smugglers and booze. Sometimes the cargo of contraband beer or liquor was carried in wooden boxes that were, in turn, placed inside bran sacks. Chased by police, rum-runners would jettison their cargo into the dark waters, and the sacks would get waterlogged and sink to the bottom. In one account from *It Happened in Prince Edward County,* a single boat carried a thousand sacks in its hold. "Just how much liquor lies on the bottom of Lake Ontario no one will ever know," the writer reckoned, "but it must be a sizeable amount."

Some days the Point is as placid as a pond. The lake seems barely to be breathing, sucking at the shoreline like an infant on a nipple. Dusty likes the lake best when it sighs in this small and rhythmic way. She is more dunker than swimmer, and she'll drive off summer heat by immersing herself up to her chest. Then she'll pass me on the shore as she scouts for something dead to roll in, and I'll catch her scent: a curry of seaweed, dog breath, wet fur, and pure doggy contentment.

There are many places at the Point to sit and ponder. The mile and a bit stretch of crown land has its own small network of two-track trails that hug the high shore, and my old Nissan truck has no trouble navigating the rolls and ruts. I know every swimming spot there, which footpaths to the water are lined with poison ivy, places off the trail to park in the shade. But the one spot I like best is the most southerly.

"You have found," David told me when I took him there, "the most private place at the entire Point."

"I love this spot," I said. "It looks like something Captain Nemo built." You may remember him as a character in the Jules Verne novel *Twenty Thousand Leagues Under the Sea*. Several bad movies help us remember the book, and my memory of Captain Nemo's submarine is of a steel hulk with many rivets, the kind of thing mad inventors built in backyard sheds in the nineteenth century. Perhaps to fortify this exposed V-shaped point and to protect the nearby lighthouse, this section of the Point features a high concrete wall on both sides of the V that faces into the lake. Two-inch-thick metal rods dangle crazily from the concrete ends like the tentacles of a squid. (A giant squid and Nemo's sub did battle, no?) Below the concrete, at the waterline, are steel plates along each side of the V. The long row of rivets, like the metal rods and the plates themselves, have turned rust brown. There's a bunker feel to Point Nemo, you have to walk a half-mile to get there from the closest parking spot, and I'm surprised that I like it so well.

But I do. The Canadian Hydrological Survey embedded a brass plate atop my favourite perch, so the place seems more about water than about war. The spot is little used, and my rock bench ten feet above the water seems the perfect place to monitor the comings and goings of wildlife. One day I sat transfixed and watched as two creatures hunted in the shallow waters below. Two moving Vs on the surface told me where they were headed, but they seemed too quick for muskrats, too small to be otters, and I was left guessing.

The show never stopped. Schools of carp, the fish two and three feet long, would lazily drift past. The water is so clear and shallow, the rock bottom so flat, that there was no missing them. Sometimes one would crest the water and I'd catch a glimpse of his bright yellow jaw. Was it a show of prowess? Was he curious? Was he eyeing me every bit as much as I was eyeing him? The call of the ducks and gulls was constant, and when the cormorants passed overhead in a line of seventy or more you could hear the fla-fla-fla of their wings. Gulls on the water rolled with the pitch of the waves, waiting for minnows drawn to the light of the sun, and, alas, for them, gulls' beaks. Offerings from a lake full of offerings.

At times like this, my troubles—such as they are—cease to exist. The inner world, that inner dialogue about what has happened or might happen, all gives way to these moments of pure spectatorship. My dog is happy to be here and I can feed a little on that; there may be ice water or a cold beer in my cooler, my pipe is at hand. I literally stop thinking. I simply am.

You can go to this spot a day later and the lake will be a roiling sea, the sky a Turner sky, the water a tropical turquoise farther out, a chalky brown near the tussled, wave-hammered shore. The concrete pad that was my seat the day before is now wet, every wave breaking over it, and even on a mid-June day you may struggle to stay warm. You can hardly think for the roar, and maybe that's why this point has been buttressed with concrete and steel, and maybe that's why I love it here. Tucked in behind the bunker, low in the grass, assaulted by the waves that rise from the cauldron below, I do not so much think as feel. The bite of the wind. The lash of the spray. The clouds racing overhead, like the mustangs I once encountered in outback Wyoming, galloping alongside the dozen horses and riders in our troupe for no reason other than pure glee.

One day I returned to my cherished lookout and was reminded that this sacred place of mine was not mine at all. Not only were people there, but they had built a fire, maybe intending to camp overnight—despite signs posted by the Ministry of Natural Resources. There are no facilities for camping here, and those who persist in staying overnight invariably leave their residue.

Sure enough, when I returned the next day, I found the spot—heretofore pristine on every occasion—sullied, though only a little. A ring of stones enclosed paper, tinfoil, and shards of glass, all blackened by fire. With some vigour and no small anger, I worked up a sweat tossing the large stones into the water below or into the bush. I then packed the foil, glass, and paper into my shoulder pack and only as I was leaving did I see the note the campers had left. It was a pencilled note, laid flat on a rock and tacked down by a circle of pebbles. By turns beseeching and threatening, it argued that the stones be left as is.

It seems "my" spot is not only used by others but has become a battleground between those who want it unsullied and those who want a barbecue pit. I know which side I'm on. Still, the note spooked me. I had visions of being interrogated by drunken pit mongers, and for weeks I found other perches on that long and craggy coast to watch the sun drop.

I was born under the sign of Pisces, the fish, and I would give a great deal to live on the water—by a great lake, a river, even a small stream. The cabin is the next best thing, close to a point surrounded on three sides by water. Water to the west, to the south, to the east. In a few minutes, I'm there.

In summer, another option at the easternmost point on that compass is a place below a steep bluff—a much underused conservation area. Here the dropoff in the water is more dramatic, and instead of limestone shelf the shore comprises flat smooth rocks the size of butter tarts. The water looks clean and is much colder than at the Point. For some reason—maybe because she can't see bottom here and can at the Point—Dusty happily retrieves sticks thrown far from shore. Or maybe it's that she's seen the Point when the lake gods are angry and doesn't trust being so far from land. She has never seen the water by the bluff turn vile.

Swimming at the bluff is almost always a semi-private affair. Even on a holiday weekend, no more than a dozen souls will be found here seeking the shade under the small trees that have obligingly rooted on the raised little shelf of land between the water on one side and the marshland on the other. An added attraction is that the place is favoured by water snakes, those creatures saddled with the reputation of being aggressive. Once at the bluff I had to dissuade children from throwing rocks at one; the snakes, I told them, are merely curious. And while I have seen some rugged thick ones curled on the shores of the Napanee River, ones I would give a wide berth to, the ones at the bluff are tiny little marvels. They miraculously disappear into black holes amid the rocks onshore, and when they swim, they are elegant beyond words, like ribbons S-ing in a lazy breeze. For hours at the bluff, they would eye us shorelings from the water, their heads and eyes protruding, their bodies dangling like useless appendages. When they had had their fill of us, they would slowly go back to business, heading determinedly north or determinedly south in search of food or wonderment and never farther from shore than I could throw a stick. They were perfect guests, curious but not too, never overstaying their welcome, and only a little vain. I hoped they thought as well of us.

Hugh Brody is a social anthropologist, filmmaker, and writer who has spent decades with hunter-gatherers in the Canadian north. During an interview with CBC Radio's *Writers & Company,* he talked about "a sense of incredible peace" that comes from spending time on the land with elders or hunters and gatherers whose knowledge of plants and animals is rooted in the specific. Inuktitut, for example, has no word for snow or bird or fish. There are words for "fresh fallen snow" and "soft snow" and "snow blowing in the wind." But nothing so bland as *snow.*

Being at the Point poses neither the risk nor the hardship of hunting and gathering on the barrens, but the solitude and the contact with creatures seem cut from the same cloth. The more time I spend at the Point, at the bluff, at the cabin, the more I am moved to embrace and know the particular. Some day I would like to be able to walk our forest and name every tree. And not just the easy ones—the white ash and the hard maple, the red oak and the shagbark hickory, the beech and the white pine. I would like to go to the Point and know, with some certainty, whether those Vs in the water are otters or muskrats or some other creature. I would know every bird on and above the water, every wildflower, every insect, and, at night, every constellation of stars, not just the Big Dipper and the Milky Way that forms a perfect arc of infinity over the cabin.

What, for example, are they called, those tiny biting flies that plague us as August draws to a close? Like pint-sized houseflies, they gather a hundred or so at a time on Dusty's back as she trots along the shoreline. So much pepper on her blond fur. Sometimes Dusty dunks her body in the lake, but the cloud patiently hovers above her and resettles the second she emerges. For lack of the proper term, I call them ankle-biters, for that is their chosen target on my body. Some days the wind drives them away. Some days the dragonflies come, hundreds and hundreds of them—as impressive as choppers hovering over a crime scene in some action film—but never enough to vanquish the ankle-biters. Thankfully, the blighters only blight for a week or so, then fade.

Early in the spring, tiny flies gather at the Point in further proof of its, of nature's, fecundity. They do not bite but rather muster in massive, Malthusian whorls—like slow-moving tornadoes. I have come to expect these displays, but every year I marvel at them.

Eustace Conway would know every bird, every wildflower, every insect, every star. He is sketched both masterfully and breezily in a book called *The Last American Man,* by Elizabeth Gilbert. Published in 2002, it takes the reader deep into the heart and mind of this gifted, charismatic, driven, and troubled man. A modern-day frontiersman.

I read the book at the cabin, in the rocking chair, early that summer, and wished it on any who cared to hear me sing its praises. It occurred to me that only times like ours—in which nature is seen by many as an alien construct, something viewed on television between car and pizza commercials—could have produced such a strange and compelling prophet. Were Eustace Conway to carry a sign, it might read "Down with materialism, back to the land!" Were he to write a book, he once said, it would be a manual called *Walk in Beauty: Living Outside.* You might arch an eyebrow at the look of him, with his buckskin clothes and moccasins, his long hair and slightly wild look, but I have the powerful sense that most of us would warm to him if we spent any time with him. We might even, as Elizabeth Gilbert did, fall for him—though likely not for long.

In the opening paragraph of *The Last American Man,* Gilbert coolly describes how, at the age of seven, Conway was successfully hunting chipmunks by throwing a knife at them and nailing them to trees. By the age of ten, he was hunting darting squirrels with a bow and arrow. Two years later, he went alone into the woods with nothing, built a shelter, and lived off the land for a week. In 1977, at the age of seventeen, he left home for good and lived in the mountains in a teepee, made fire by rubbing sticks together, and dressed himself in animal skins.

Conway was born in South Carolina. Behind his family's suburban home was an old-growth forest, with quicksand and bears and snakes—some poisonous. Conway's father would take him back there and name each plant, bird, and animal they encountered. His mother, a capable rider and at home in the woods, taught him how to build a fire, gut game, weave grass into rope, and sew buckskin. *Wild Wood Wisdom* was the sort of book she urged on him.

The Conways were, without knowing it, equipping their son for future adventures, such as hiking, at the age of nineteen, the two-thousand-mile Appalachian Trail, surviving pretty well on what he could hunt and gather. There was also, in 1995, his mad dash on horseback across the United States, setting a world record along the way. He did it in 103 days, at a fifty-mile-a-day clip. I've done some backcountry riding, in Wyoming and Alberta, and I can tell you that riding at that pace is akin to running marathons one after the other. Doing the distance is hard enough; keeping your horse fed and watered, fit, and injury free is at least half the battle. What is even more astonishing is that Conway never grew up with horses and owned his first one only ten years ago; he acquired his degree in horsemanship at about the same speed he raced across the continent.

Eustace Conway would become famous in some circles as the high priest of connectedness—"the CEO of the woods," Gilbert tags him. He would fashion a living by conveying to others his frontier knowledge and, somehow, come to own a thousand-acre stretch of pristine wilderness called Turtle Island—a kind of sacred summer camp where he would teach doting pilgrims what he called "the high art and godliness of nature." The wide-eyed are taught to wield knives, carve their own wooden spoons, what to eat in the forest, and the joy that comes with the ritual of rising at dawn to meditate before the rising sun.

Gilbert understands full well, or thinks she does, the depression and anxiety that mark our culture. She refers to our "profound alienation. We have fallen out of rhythm. It's this simple ... we seem to have stopped paying attention." Eustace Conway would lament as he made his rounds of high schools that only one child in fifty understands the notion of sacredness.

He must sigh at all this, as no doubt Walt Whitman did in his day. The poet had served as a volunteer nurse for the Union army during the American Civil War, an experience that came close to shattering him. He was old before his time and partially paralyzed, and he would have fallen into absolute poverty were it not for patrons overseas and in his homeland. Whitman was a man of simple needs, and a prophet in the way that Eustace Conway is a prophet. A few listen to the prophets and even toss coins at them, but men like Whitman and Conway are mostly ignored.

Whitman once asked—and this was a century ago—where his country's manic surge forward was headed. "After you have exhausted what there is in business, politics, conviviality, and so on—what remains?" he asked, and then answered: "Nature remains."

One hopes.

A psychologist might say that a private point of land jutting out into water has a hold on me because of my childhood. I was raised mostly in a Scarborough bungalow that seems cramped only in retrospect. One of my favourite spots while I lived there was the Scarborough Bluffs, three-hundred-twenty-eight-feet-high cliffs that overlook Lake Ontario. I still like the ripples of energy that come from family gatherings, from parties and crowds, from noise and chaos, but I also seek escape from all that. In a packed room, I confess to suffering from mild claustrophobia, and all my life I have been a light sleeper. The older I get, the more I crave space and light and quiet. The cabin and the Point fill that bill nicely. It seems important that I take a ferry to get to the cabin, and though the trip across Adolphus Reach may last no more than ten minutes, it fosters the illusion that I've come to an island. A world apart.

The Point appeals because it's rarely the same experience two days in a row. The quality of light changes from day to day, from season to season. A painter friend, Susan Straiton, says it was the light that drew her to live here, close by the Point, and she makes a modest living, in part, by capturing the Point at its most dramatic. Ulrike and I bought one of her smaller works, one that shows the Point in mid-winter: great pans of ice as far as the eye can see, some shelves in the distance tilted to form little mountain ranges, some broken pieces caught in vertical pose at the shore, like jagged quartz. The scene looks like something Sir John Franklin might have witnessed from the decks of the *Erebus* or *Terror* in their doomed expedition to the High Arctic in 1847.

The painting has a name, "Ice Shears," and though the medium is oil, the work is so precise that the feel is keenly photographic. Most observers are fooled. Even the sky seems true, caught in a real moment.

Too seldom do we look up. The Point insists that I do. All through that summer of 2002 the skies over southeastern Ontario were invariably blue, the colour of drought. August had less rain than any August since the provincial government began recording rainfall. But in the fall, the clouds began to roll in and with them fall rains. The sky got interesting again. One day at the Point early in September, I saw cirrus clouds with long trailers—"mare's tails"—a sky much like the one in Susan Straiton's painting. But there were also thunderclouds, then would come a break and the sun would cast a brilliant silver sheen on the iron grey waters.

The waves seemed to roll in slow motion—as if for dramatic effect. Gather, roll. Gather, roll. The wind, meanwhile, was a rippling thing that tore at the pages of my notebook, ruffled my T-shirt, and snapped my pants at the ankles. A batten-down-the hatch wind. A nor'wester. A dull roar of a wind.

It felt good to face into all that weather, like a ship's prow into a storm. At times like this I wish I could convey what I felt on a canvas, or in music, instead of mere words. The sky was so vast I would need a football field for my mural, an opera score were I a composer.

Sometimes a duck would pass in front of me, heading north, and I had to admire his pluck. The pluck of a wind-tossed duck. He would tack, like a sailor, and press on, as if late for some important meeting.

Friends of ours actually live near the Point, back up the coast a little to the northwest. Mounted on their living room wall is one of Susan Straiton's more epic paintings of the Point in full fury, the breakers like something you might see at the ocean's shore, an offshore wind skimming every wave top as wind and water spar. I have stood by that massive painting, torn between it and the view out the door to the sunroom from where the real thing could be seen in motion. Torn between the static and what looked to be surreal. Some days, the work of art and the work of the gods are almost identical and, as powerful as the painting is, it is the real thing that beckons. Were I to live in that house, I would accomplish nothing, but only stare as if out to sea, like a woman on a widow's walk compelled to watch the water for signs of a mast on the horizon.

I am intrigued by the notion of exploring the Point, and the coast beyond, from the water. On calm days the canoe would manage the near shore, but I dare not go farther. The lake can change its mind in a hurry. One summer day, when the waves were fierce at the Point, Kurt and I took the canoe out into the roiling surf and played this raucous game: walk the canoe straight out, five or ten waves out, while the water fights us for control, and, between waves, jump in and ride the surf to shore. It was comical how easily the canoe tipped. Our visitor from France, Pierre-Édouard, joined us for a time but soon lost his appetite for the game. He swims all summer long in the English Channel, but these waves unnerved him.

If I do explore county coastlines, I will hug that shore and there'll be life jackets on board. I would rather not join the *Julia* and the *Persia*, the *Jessie* and the other wrecks all those fathoms down. I love the water a lot and fear it not a little.

In November, the water at the Point recedes and the flat expanse of moss-covered rock reveals itself. Nature tidies up. Zebra mussel shells by the millions all get swept to the high tide mark, some fifty feet beyond the waterline. Huge flat rocks are deposited, sometimes artfully, where the shore ends and high ground starts its rise. Wind-driven water, mighty as it is, has as yet not powered these rocks up the hill, but I am astonished to see that all the heavy pieces I threw in anger here and there from the Captain Nemo heights are now, four months later, on their edges and neatly gathered.

My visits to the Point are short in November. Even my cherished place looks a little forlorn in this, the bleakest of months. Birds are few, just lingering sandpipers and buffleheads. Amid the many pools of water left by the receding lake lies the carcass of a once great bullfrog. He is turned on his back, legs splayed in cruel indignity, throat cut into and mouth yawning but otherwise intact. Even on this bright mild day he seems to capture the mood of the grey month.

"Hewers of wood, drawers of water." It was a phrase that some political economists used, and still use, to mock their fellow Canadians over our apparent failure to modernize and up our manufacturing capacity. The lament was that we relied too heavily on the great gift of our natural resources, which we sold raw to other countries—the United States primarily—leaving them to turn the wood and minerals into furniture, cars, and other finished goods.

If that charge were ever accurate, I am guilty of it yet. I still hew wood, still haul water. "Simplicity, simplicity, simplicity," Thoreau urged. "Hairshirt, hairshirt, hairshirt," I heard him say. Mine is the plain and simple sanctuary. There are sinks, all right, in what passes for kitchen and bathroom, but whatever water falls into the grey-water system I built just to the west of the cabin has been hauled here in five-gallon jugs.

For years I put off hooking up our well to the cabin—in part because the well promised so little water, in part because introducing running water is so expensive. Pump, plumbing, lines, air tanks, faucets: the choice was between bringing a few jugs of water each trip to the cabin and laying out several thousand dollars I did not possess. For years, I have hauled heavy jugs of water. From the bed of the truck to the kitchen sink, and up the stairs to what I dare to call the bathroom (a sink from a recycling depot set into varnished plywood and supported by a frame of two-by-fours). And the business of water hauling seems to have induced a water conservancy practice.

I called a plumber to the cabin a few years ago. He and his apprentice wrestled a six hundred-gallon plastic holding tank into the basement, but only after temporarily removing the stairs first.

"At the rate we use water," I told the plumber, "one tank will likely last us the summer."

A wiry young man with an almost cocky air, he assured me that every family—once spared the rigour of hauling water—soon reverts to wasteful use. We discussed the pros and cons of hooking up the well, of drawing rainwater off the roof and making the holding tank into a kind of cistern, of calling in the water trucks (at seventy-five dollars a load), of maybe doing all three—each a supplement to the other during the dry summers that seem to be in the offing for most of us. In winter, there being no furnace, the system would have to be drained, and I would revert to my role as water hauler. The plumber left, promising he'd be in touch.

But that summer, a drought plagued the county. When I called him, the plumber said he was too busy attending to farmers desperate to water their cattle and to homeowners whose wells had run dry. And if he never called back after that, neither did I call him. Old habits die hard, and I simply went on hauling water. For years the tank sat in the basement. At Thanksgiving one year, my tiny nephews and nieces used it as a kind of playground slide. Running water would come to the cabin one day, but it would take its time. In the meantime, I have what you might call walking water.

In summer, I can drive the truck right to the cabin's back door and haul my several water jugs into the house. The wheelbarrow can also be pressed into service. A rain barrel married to the downspout at the cabin's northwest corner supplies water for the solar shower, several tomato plants, and any young trees in need of a drink. (Made of heavy plastic and outfitted with tap, overflow hose, and sturdy mesh top to keep mosquitoes out, the rain barrel once housed Greek olive oil.) In winter, the driveway thick with snow, I park the truck at the road and load the jugs and my other supplies onto a toboggan. Were the distance longer than it is, I suppose Dusty could always be put into harness and to work (she is part husky, after all). But she would rather play, running at a goodly clip and scooping up snow in her jaws as she goes.

As for actually dispensing the water inside the cabin, at first I made do with the blue plastic jug with spiggot that we had used while camping. Then I chanced upon a more elegant alternative—ceramic dispensers. You can find them at stores that specialize in spring water trappings, though mine came more cheaply. One at a yard sale, for five dollars, the other free, from Oma. Both are made serviceable by simply turning a water jug upside down into the yawning ceramic barrel. Jug and dispenser reside at the edge of the sink, and one can tell at a glance when the supply is low. As for operating the device, spiggot and gravity do the job.

There is no hot water, of course. In the manner of the Europeans, who do not keep a supply of hot water on hold as we do, but heat it as needed, I boil water in a kettle for use in the bathroom-to-be upstairs or at the kitchen sink downstairs. Maybe it is the contrarian in me that sticks with these customs, or maybe it is this: the more the cabin is fitted with the trappings of home, the less it can lay claim to separateness and that distinguishing title of sanctuary.

For some of the same reasons, I have also resisted installing a septic system. Warned that such a system would cost five thousand dollars or more, I have kept the privy rather than install modern plumbing. If anything, I am leaning toward a composting toilet and not the flushing kind. Something tells me that I will go on using the privy even *after* the toilet of our choosing is bolted down. As for grey water from the kitchen, it drains out into a simple underground leaching pit. The thing is described, and artfully, in a book called *Cottage Water Systems,* by Max Burns.

Imagine a small fort, eight feet by six feet, made of concrete blocks and filled with gravel, the whole affair buried a foot under grass level. The plastic PVC pipe from the kitchen ends in the midst of the gravel, so that stone, earth, and sand do the work of filtering and cleaning the water on its meandering path to underground lakes and streams. Eventually, the gravel supply will have to be replaced, but my sense is that that's years and years down the road. Max Burns is convinced, as I am, that grey water and sewage should be treated separately. Grease and soap simply gum up septic fields, and so the plan is to ease modern toiletry into life at the cabin, while continuing to deploy pit and privy.

In due time, or plumber's time, the waterworks at the cabin will get a new face.

I love water, as I say, yet I fear it. Not so much death by drowning (though were you to see me swim you might wonder how I've avoided such a fate) but another kind of death, slow but sure. Water is the great enemy of all wood houses—especially hewn log houses. Charles McRaven, an American expert on the subject and a longtime contractor in the field, tells of a cabin that periodically faced wind-driven rain from the southwest, rain that invaded every crack in the wood, every flaw in the chinking, every tiny hole left by powderpost beetles. He and his crew resorted to caulking massively and then painting that whole side with creosote, engine oil, and bleach oil—a drastic weatherproofing measure that at least retained the structure's natural grey colour. (My own research—looking on the Internet under "organic alternatives to treated lumber"—turned up this more benign recipe: one and a half cups of boiled linseed oil, one ounce melted paraffin or wood rosin wax, and enough mineral spirits to make up a gallon. The concoction darkens the logs, but only slightly.)

Sometimes McRaven uses a mason's pointing tool to drive fibreglass into a cabin's thin cracks, then uses the same tool to push in plaster overtop. It can require endless detective work to determine which crack lets in water and which does not, and one must err on the dry side of caution. Some owners of pioneer dwellings give up the fight and simply apply a cover of board and batten to troublesome exterior walls; some build wraparound porches on the south and west side to fend off both sun and rain. Some log house restorers shrug their shoulders, insisting that the log cabin was never meant to exist anywhere other than in the woods where the trees block the wind and ease the problem of driving rain. A cabin in a windswept field, like mine, they say, is bound to leak. Better start planting trees all around the cabin, they say with a smirk.

The tricky business of closing the gaps in old log houses—of shutting out the wind and the cold and the rain—is one reason so many log buildings endured at all. Some got covered in clapboard the minute they were built, or later, because hewn log had fallen out of fashion. But many owners—weary of chinking, weary of gaps, aware that rain-soaked wood is an open invitation to bugs and rot—simply covered up with tarpaper, clapboard, stucco, brick, or, as in the case of our own cabin, board and batten. Sometimes log buildings lay swathed in these protective shields for a century or more, waiting patiently for someone to come along who was keen enough, brave enough, foolish enough to let the old lodgings see the sun (and rain) again.

And to close those gaps. I am reminded of a poem by Scottish poet Alastair Reid about an obsessive man he called "the o-filler." The man would go to libraries and, with a pencil, fill in every *o* in every book he could lay his hands on. It had become his life's work, something he did daily and, he was sure, with increasing panache and efficiency. Some days it feels like my mission in life is weatherproofing the Bresee cabin. The gap-filler understands the o-filler all too well. Ours are both tales of obsession.

Fall rains sometimes see the cabin leaking, anew, and with vigour, on that south side. The south side has already been rechinked once owing to calamitous leaks that first spring and the discovery that the chinking crew had somehow (!) forgotten to insulate between logs along that entire wall. Only Michael and I poking around behind the grout (to fathom the leaks) had revealed that severe oversight. I fretted then, got over my fretting, and did not fret for years, then suffered a mild relapse in the fall of 2002.

I fretted about the puddles that formed on the floor after heavy driving rain from the south. About the mice that had returned after an absence of years (blasts of wind twice blowing open doors in the night may have put down a red carpet for the cute little chewers, which peak in seven-year cycles and this was the Year of the Mouse). About the complicated set of stairs I wanted to replace the "temporary" steep set Michael had built, about the porch and the pond, the composting toilet, and the solar power installation I had in mind. For years the cabin simply *was,* a place built of worry, but then had come the years-long payoff. The cabin had brought me a sense of peace and relief and calm. Suddenly I felt a powerful (male menopausal?) urge to protect and improve, make better.

Still, the chinking was my real source of worry. Rereading the McRaven book had planted new fears. There's an art, you see, to chinking. When done improperly or when pushed out by expanding logs, chinking can actually create an easy route for water to enter the logs and, eventually, to rot them by pooling inside. The more water that comes in, by turns freezing and thawing, the more the chinking pushes out and traps yet more water: the damage feeds on itself.

McRaven uses a pointing trowel to tuck the mortar in and under exterior logs, then slopes the mortar down and out at the bottom so it's flush with the log below. Rainwater is thus shed from one row of chinking to the next and coaxed to the ground. "The tucked-in slope" is an ingenious and simple matter, for McRaven, anyway. But every year he rechinks log houses, some recently chinked but badly. McRaven also recommends in his book that the cement be waterproofed with two coats of clear exterior masonry sealer. Had we done that? Why not? Was the cabin going to fall down around my ears?

I was even doubting the chinking material itself. The pioneers used moss or mud, clay or horsehair; French pioneers, who built log walls by laying the logs vertically and rooting them in the earth or on sills of rock, chinked with what they called *bouzillage*—clay or mud fortified with straw, twigs, or animal hair. (In one old cabin in northern Ontario, the spaces between logs were found to be stuffed with all manner of cloth, including someone's long underwear.) Modern chinking mixes deploy mélanges of clay, lime, fibreglass, or plastic. McRaven's personal choice is much like masonry mortar (one part lime, two parts Portland cement, and nine parts sand to achieve an authentic-looking light grey). What mix had we used? Over the years, as the logs had settled and cracks revealed themselves, I had patched using a modern synthetic chinking compound, but McRaven warns that most are petroleum-based plastic—which eventually breaks down in sunlight. And no wall, of course, gets more sunlight and just plain weather than that south wall. I fretted about all this and was reminded of that eighteenth-century phrase, "It is not the work that kills, but worry." And I was keenly aware of the irony in worrying about that which gave me peace of mind.

I thought of something I had read in Bruce Chatwin's *Songlines* years ago. He was arguing then that the wanderer is infinitely happier than the sedentary man, who always insists on change and is the prisoner of his possessions. In the Australian desert, Chatwin had encountered an Irish hermit priest named Father Terence who lived in a hut with a typewriter and little else. He was writing a manual on poverty and his advice, as Chatwin recorded it, was to live without things. "Things filled men with fear," Chatwin had him saying. "The more things they had, the more they had to fear. Things had a way of riveting themselves onto the soul and then telling the soul what to do."

I read somewhere that anthropologists have studied hunter-gatherer societies all over the world. What they found is that individuals carried with them on their forays no more than twenty-five pounds worth of gear. Anything more was deemed superficial.

For all the cabin's rustic feel, it still makes demands on me. It is a special thing, but still, one more *thing* that requires maintenance, repair, time, thought, money. And sometimes the cabin causes me a wagonload of fretting.

I'm sitting at a round table in a hewn log house and admiring the place when Sandy MacLachlan steps in as if he owned it (which, at one time, he did). He's an impish man of seventy-eight years, five feet, two inches tall, with a strong nose and a lively manner. Joey Smallwood without the swagger. A red checked shirt under a navy blue trenchcoat, a square briefcase to suggest a man quietly going about his business.

He grew up in Kingston and the Ottawa Valley and ran a lumber business, as his father had done before him. One of his favourite expressions is "by gum!" and if he's unsure about the species of wood in hand, he will chew it to make a final determination.

I show him a photo album depicting our cabin in various stages of construction, and he can tell right away—by the straightness of the logs—that it's white pine. MacLachlan very much admires the cabin and the obvious skill of its original builders, but he prefers eastern white cedar. Though it bows and dips and lacks the neatness of white pine, he loves it for its durability, its light weight, and its smell when freshly cut.

The building we're sitting in now, he says, waving his arms over his head, was built of eastern white cedar in 1853. It's a thirty-by-twenty-four-foot storey-and-a-half building, dimensionally almost identical to the cabin I call mine. Today the cedar building houses the MacLachlan Woodworking Museum just west of Kingston, and hundreds of pioneer building tools. Some six thousand students, tourists, and locals visit every year. "People fall into things," MacLachlan says to explain how he came to build the museum, and I understood immediately what he meant, having fallen into things myself.

"My great-grandfather," he continues, "lived in a log house. And when I was a kid, I played with Canadian Logs as toys. But that doesn't really explain my fascination with old log houses. People get deeply, emotionally involved with old log houses. Maybe it's because wood is a living organism. Is it because," and he laughs at his own joke, "we're descended from monkeys who sought protection in trees? I don't know." Sandy MacLachlan only knows that people don't fall for aluminum bungalows as they do for historic wood houses.

One day in 1966 while travelling between Ottawa and Kingston, MacLachlan was admiring all the old log buildings in the valley and he had this notion—a notion that would become a centennial project to mark the nation's birth—of a museum to celebrate wood. And what better place to do that than in a pioneer log house? He began to scout for a likely home for his burgeoning collection of antique tools acquired at country auctions and from generous donors. He would go cruising around the Ottawa Valley on Saturdays and eventually compiled what he called "a logbook" of some fifty-nine buildings, with pictures, dimensions and details, and the names of their owners.

The house that MacLachlan settled on was built in 1853 by a man named Robert White who lived there with his wife, Jane, and their six daughters and four sons. The ground floor was equally divided, with partitions to create kitchen, dining room, parlour, and parents' bedroom, with the upstairs loft separated into two bedrooms—one for the boys, one for the girls.

The eldest son, William White, should have inherited the house—as was then the custom—but, owing to a conflict between father and son, William received nothing in his father's will but the pointedly meagre sum of one dollar. The second-eldest boy, a shy and nervous fellow named Richard, inherited the homestead and allowed younger siblings to live with him. He never married and eventually lived in the cabin alone, making a kind of living as an apothecary preparing cures for eczema and nosebleeds until he died in 1918.

His sister, Elizabeth, and her husband had bought the land on which the cabin stood in 1914—"for love and affection" and for the nominal sum of one dollar. Four years later, another family, the Wilsons, bought the house and set it up as a dance hall to supplement the family income. Later owners moved it (the current location of the house is its fourth site) and modified it slightly, and the last family to live in it, the Lackies, abandoned it in 1946. For twenty years it lay vacant, until Sandy MacLachlan gave it new life. This is the brief history of the building we now sit in while light snow drifts down outside in November of 2002.

MacLachlan has a theory that old wood is a hardier creature than new wood. "I have," he says, "two beams in my house"—a hewn house he found near the village of Numogate northeast of Kingston in the early 1970s. "They're white pine and the growth rings are so tiny you need a magnifying glass to see them. Those trees faced intense competition, so they grew slowly." MacLachlan is convinced that slow growth converts to strength and durability. That may be the bias of a latter-day Canadian timber baron, but MacLachlan politely dismisses what he calls "Appalachian oak." He describes its growth rings of five-eighths of an inch, and contrasts that with the one-eighth-of-an-inch growth rings of local oak. In both cases, each ring represents a year's growth. "There *must* be a difference in strength," he says.

But as much as I share Sandy's respect and admiration for old wood, I also worry about my old wood under the assault of driving rain. How to protect that south wall?

"You could experiment," offered Sandy. "Try a water sealant on one section and see if that works against wind-driven rain. You can also fill in the really big checks [wide cracks in the wood]. I darken the caulk with a bit of ash from the fire."

"What about a porch?" I countered. Sandy visibly winced.

"Porches on cabins, that was more of an American thing," he said. Translation: Sandy MacLachlan isn't quite the purist he once was, but he still squirms at the notion of an American porch on a Canadian cabin.

Later, I would come upon a book called *Early Life in Upper Canada* and learn that the first settlers' homes in Ontario were erected along the Detroit River by disbanded French soldiers in the final decades of French rule in Canada. Built of logs, pine boards, or stone, the *habitants*' neat cottages were low affairs with steep roofs and wide eaves. One observer called the French Canadian's home "a little house *with verandahs all around* [my italics], few windows and few fancies; everything done with an air of humble comfort."

No, the more I pondered a porch, the more I liked it and the less I liked the other options. Sealants only work for a year or two before ultraviolet light begins to break them down. The ongoing expense and labour, and the thought of brushing a chemical on those wonderful old logs, seemed both nonsensical and heretical. I could plant trees in the meantime as a buffer to wind and rain—and my great-grandchildren, should they come and should the cabin endure that long, could enjoy their protective shade. But too many trees would take away the long view, down the middle field to the south field and the one beyond, a view I cherish.

No, a porch was shaping in my mind. I had seen such porches, American porches, on old square-timbered cabins, and, frankly, I liked them. The porch took away nothing from the cabin's authenticity, and even enhanced it. I could easily imagine the Bresee/Scanlan cabin with one. I could see the cedar shakes on top, pine posts holding up the porch, the cedar decking. I could see the wood greying in the sun, the rocking chair on the porch. Me in the rocker. Coffee in hand. Admiring the morning. And not worried at all about the forecast of heavy rain and wild wind from the south.

One clear cold winter day I drove through the Ottawa Valley for a gathering of Canadian horse lovers in Pakenham, and I spotted a square-timbered house of my cabin's vintage right on Highway 29. I stopped for a closer look. A wide porch fronted the place, with a rocking chair in one corner and tin roof overtop. It seemed to suit the cabin fine. As I drove on, I noticed more porches, gracing two and even three sides of Victorian farmhouses. The porches posed no affront to the architecture, even added a certain panache. I imagined the owners moving from east to south to western exposures—coffee in the morning, tea in the afternoon, wine at sunset, following the light as sunflowers do. The long drive home seemed to go quickly for me, porch-possessed as I then was.

By midsummer, the cabin got its porch and I was a porch-proud man. It was built by a local carpenter named Peter Blendell, built well, with sturdy square posts of six-inch pine, decking of western cedar, and two skylights lined up over the windows to minimize the inevitable darkening of interiors that is the price of porches. I had thought I would work with Peter and his crew and that at least decking and roofing would fall to me. But writing about the cabin conflicted with working on the cabin, and so Peter and an eager crew of county lads built the porch, a simple lean-to but elegant in its way.

"It feels so expansive," I said to David and his partner, Karen, as Peter joined us one evening for a celebratory beer on the porch. From the cabin wall to the edge of the porch measured more than eight feet.

"Expensive?" David asked.

"Yes, that too," I conceded.

I had only that day seen the porch for the first time and, as we sat in chairs looking south across the fields and the long shadows cast by the round bales that Farmer Guernsey had that day gathered up, a coyote crossed in front of the hedgerow a stone's throw away. He was tawny grey and russet brown and, though he was no bigger than Dusty, he did not walk with her daisy-cutter trot but with great power and purpose. He was moving east and the sun caught his colours and lasered them into my memory bank. I took his appearance as an omen and was certain that if I sat on that porch long enough and was watchful enough at all hours, I would see more of the same.

The porch was project number two that year. The winter before—the hard winter that began in such desultory fashion, then puffed up its chest as the new year broke and hung on far too long into 2003—the cabin finally got its proper stairs, the ones my architect pal Robert Gregoire had so generously designed. By the end of February, I could say, *"L'escalier Gregoire, c'est fini."* Started in the mild weather of December, the stairs were built in January and early February during the coldest days that winter could muster. There were days when the driveway filled in and the carpenters (Peter Blendell and his gifted cohort, Robert Wiens), had to haul in wood and tools on a toboggan.

I had come to engage Peter in a roundabout way, after asking a cabinetmaker friend in the county if he had any interest in the job. No, he said, too busy, but he highly recommended Peter, who lived at the edge of the village not ten minutes down our road. A little shy, but fussy (he's semi-retired and only takes work he enjoys), he reminded me a lot of Michael. But unlike Michael, who always had to cut his own path as he strived to marry old wood and new, Peter had a blueprint to work from as he fashioned our stairs. Indeed, he would later say, a very fine blueprint.

What had started as a joke over dinner at the cabin one night ("Hey Bob, why don't you draw us up a proper set of stairs?")

resulted in blueprints about a year later. Rough notes from his visit to the cabin had occupied a corner of his office at home (no doubt engulfed by paper, dust, and eraser rubble—what a friend of mine used to call "desk smegma"). I assumed that Bob had forgotten the project. Then one evening he phoned to say he needed some extra measurements. As always, I was thinking rough sketch—a loose drawing we could pass on to a carpenter. But what came in the mail was a hand-drawn, five-part, three-page document on eleven-by-seventeen-inch graph paper. Overheads, side view, details of supports in the basement for the heavy pine beam the stair would pivot around. Every minute detail of riser and tread, of stair winders and stair nosings—all had been drawn in Bob's careful hand. Fine black felt pen, all the words in caps.

I looked at the blueprint and instinctively liked it, but I couldn't imagine its actual shape. Ulrike, with her designer's eye, had a better handle on it. As for Peter, he joined us at the cabin one day, took about thirty seconds to look at the blueprint, eyed the space, and said "Yeah, we can do this."

In fact, he said, we (he and his fellow carpenter) might get it done by Christmas. That deadline was missed. Flu, holidays, weather, circumstance—all intervened. Weeks became months and my separation anxiety deepened: I had never gone so long without spending a night at the cabin. The delays reminded me of the old days, the dark days when it seemed that the cabin was only crawling to completion.

But I had a good feeling about Peter, and I worried about him working in that stone cold cabin, arriving there in the early morning with the gauge inside locked on minus twenty-five. I brought some space heaters to the cabin, along with a circulating oil heater (it looks like a small radiator and, though powered by electricity, is far more energy efficient than space heaters). Turns out it was the woodstove and the little computer fans that Peter had the most praise for. I sometimes malign that stove and its tiny box; now I felt almost proud of it.

In an e-mail, Peter had said the stairs worked out "pretty good." He was being polite. I loved how they tucked so modestly into that southeast corner, how the rippling grain of the ash introduced a vibrant new wood into the cabin with all its old and new pine. Best, the stairs looked as if they belonged, like they'd always been there. I looked forward to coating them with the same mixture of spar varnish, linseed oil, and solvent I had used on the soap box. The heavy pine post would be allowed to grey and join—at least in spirit—its nineteenth-century cousins.

Near the end of February and for the first time in almost three months, I spent two nights at the cabin. An ice storm had struck just days before and now the land, every tree and shrub, was encased in glass. I cannot remember a brighter day in my life. An image came to me of Inuit in centuries past walking the barrens and avoiding snow blindness by wearing wraparound eye shields with tiny horizontal slits.

The low winter sun poured into the cabin that day. I sat at the table in the southwest corner, reading and jotting down notes, but I could not take my eyes off those stairs. I liked how hefty they felt underfoot, not a creak as you passed over them. The noonday sun would cast intricate shadows on the steps, the window's muntins adding to the show. As the sun veered west, the elegant crosshatching would crawl up the stairs. Eventually, I stopped looking at the stairs and sat on them, pleased that I had a new vantage from which to view cabin and grounds.

What grounds they were that day. At noon, at sunset, on both days, I succumbed to Dusty's pleading eyes and walked the pup south across the field and then north again toward the forest. Every blade of tall grass poking out of the deep snow, every branch of every tree wore a thick coat of silver. If I knocked the grass, I would hear the sound of breaking glass. And though the snow was several feet deep, a layer of ice below an inch or so of snow cover easily took our weight. No slogging. Hiking was a breeze. I had worn nylon shin and ankle covers anticipating a tramp, but this was like walking on water.

I wondered how some of the trees we had planted west of the cabin had fared in the ice storm and was dismayed to note that many locusts had either lost a major limb or broken at the crown. That quick growth had come at a price, and as I surveyed the damage I thought of Sandy MacLachlan's words in praise of slow growth. Still, it was the sterling beauty of the trees that gave me pause, not these losses. I kept staring up, gawking as I have done in medieval cathedrals. There was a subtle music in the air. I thought I could hear ice cubes in tall glasses, small Tibetan bells and wind chimes, water dripping in a cave—though it was well below freezing.

The fresh snowfall told of just how much animal traffic courses through the fields and in and around the hedgerows. I could see where the rabbits had congregated under a certain sumach, I followed the meandering path of deer and was struck by the size of paw prints I took to be those of coyotes, though the prints were very large. Dusty took special interest in these. She buried her nose in one and left it there for half a minute, trying to conjure its maker, its maker's sex, age, and vitality. Her behaviour was akin to that of a wine connoisseur looking for that hint of oak or cherry or licorice in a vintage wine. Urine in the snow was doubly of interest, and she would go back to the same spot each time we were in the neighbourhood. In the forest we disturbed a hawk, and when the great bird vacated his aviary, ice and snow fell heavily to the ground. Under a small conifer lay a thick patch of black hair, like horsehair, and I wondered what remains we would find here in the spring. Back in the field I noticed many arrow-shaped tracks I took to be those of birds, maybe crows. I could see where one had walked east, then north, and south again, then rose and maybe repeated his indecision in the air.

Back at the cabin, I swept up the fine sawdust—remnants of ash and oak and pine—that had coated every inch of the place I had not draped in plastic sheeting back in December. Sweeping the cabin always makes me feel good, like tidying my desk at home when the desk smegma has become too thick, like catching up on correspondence or phoning the old folks on a Saturday morning: small duties with disproportionate rewards.

In late spring, I connected once more with Sandy MacLachlan. He had promised me a tour of his old log house on the St. Lawrence River—only minutes from the woodworking museum that bears his name—and I held him to it.

Truly a log house (*cabin* fails to capture its grandeur), it sits on a high granite promontory and commands a splendid view looking northeast down the river. A crow bearing in that direction would in time find the way to Quebec City. Home to Sandy and Ruth MacLachlan is actually a tidy merger of two log houses, both built around 1850. If you count the garage, the little guest house, a utility shed in progress, and the wood hut, there are actually *six* hewn log buildings of varying size on Sandy's property. This is hewn house heaven and Sandy MacLachlan is head keeper and builder.

He tells me that he has a guest book, which he asks all who have stayed either for a meal or a night's lodging to sign. There are more than one thousand entries in the book (the MacLachlan family has been on this point since 1930), so I am by no means the first to have been granted the grand tour. Sandy's method is the same for each building: circle it, admire it from outside, tell its story in detail by way of honouring its past, then enter. He pays particular attention to the chinking on each building, and he is partial to the lime and sand mix that was used on many of Kingston's old limestone buildings.

As we circled the main house, the first thing that struck me as I gazed up was the exaggerated soffit, or overhang, of the roof. If Sandy had few worries about wind-driven rain, here was one of the keys. Where the soffit on my vulnerable cabin was a foot wide at best, Sandy had surrounded his house with two and a half feet of soffit. "Swiss and Nordic countries had big overhangs to protect their buildings," he told me, ever didactic, "and so a two-hundred-year-old log building in Scandinavia is nothing special." Factor in the shield of coniferous and deciduous trees on the south, east, and west of Sandy's house, plus the natural resistance of eastern white cedar to water, and you would have to believe that many of his hewn houses will still be on that point a hundred and fifty years from now.

My own cabin, the Bresee cabin, had been rebuilt quite precisely to mimic the style prevalent in 1827 when it was first built. Sandy called it a Georgian fashion, with a dominant dormer on the presenting side, windows flanking it, and a small overhang—in the manner of British stone buildings of the day. It wasn't that builders were unaware of the folly of small overhangs; it was more that the log cabin was seen as a temporary building. I repeat: those that have endured often do so courtesy of long periods under protective siding.

Sandy MacLachlan's faith in old wood and his pure passion for heritage objects (Ruth shares his besottedness) has been passed on to his three children. Around the bay, son Ross and family live in a hundred-and-fifty-year-old log house (but with modern touches, such as a green steel roof and an imposing arched window overlooking the river). Like father, like son, and small wonder.

Inside what is now a guest cabin—it served as the family cottage for decades—Sandy sat down at a small ornate organ built in 1892 and played a song his mother had taught him, "Long Long Ago." It was a gleeful performance. We had previously paused at the door to admire the ornate black door knocker, one that came from a stone cottage in Kingston much used by Sir John A. Macdonald. The cabin's stair rail is a piece of black walnut rescued from a tree before it was felled to make way for a highway; the handrail is rustic, though polished by linseed oil and the thousand or so hands that have held it, and it matches the place perfectly.

Sandy MacLachlan has come a long way from the early days when he began to collect antiques. The first piece he ever bought was what he then proudly called "a one-handled soup tureen," a phrase that amused older, wiser onlookers at the auction that day who knew a chamber pot when they saw one. The guest cabin and the main house have become repositories for myriad antique china tea sets, antique corner cupboards of butternut and pine, dozens of antique oil lamps, antique wooden spoons. This is only a little of what you can see, but every cupboard, every drawer also teems with old things.

In later years, Sandy would hunt for hand-wrought strap hinges and find them in the long grass by chicken houses. He would learn the language of pioneer history, about latch bars, keepers and strikers, thumb-latches, hanging corner cupboards. He would scout for derelict cabins, collect the best old square-timbered logs, and stack them on his point of land. One never knew when one would need another hewn house. For a lover of wood, as Sandy MacLachlan surely is, every tall white pine about to be felled, every old barn or old house slated for demolition has him licking his chops. I think the hunt keeps him young.

The main house's hefty crossbeam, for example, was plucked from a barn north of Kingston. Originally forty feet long and measuring twelve inches by twelve inches, this glorious white pine—to judge by its tiny growth rings—may well have been alive when Columbus arrived in the New World.

Sandy MacLachlan is not quite the purist you would think. He has occasionally removed old paint from antiques, defying the current fashion to leave it on. And there's a playfulness, an inventiveness about him that I find charming. It's there in the child-size, three-legged cherrywood stool he made for the guest cabin, the homemade white pine chairs, the transom sashes he fashions out of old windows, and, especially, the laundry chute he devised. I laughed out loud at his clever rig: the clothes get tossed into the chute (disguised by wallpaper) on the second floor and they land one storey below on a wide pine board held in place by ropes and Sandy's handmade wooden keeper, which is, in turn, attached to a drop string and wooden handle. Ruth pulls down on that Murphy bed arrangement and the clothes tumble directly into the washing machine; a pulley attached to a rock resets the contraption.

Of all the stories he told that day, the one that Sandy enjoyed telling most concerned the old six-panelled door he found at Pollitt's, a used building supply dealer north of Kingston. I have found the odd treasure hunting there amid the castoff sinks and demolition lumber, but pickings must have been better in bygone days. Sandy found there an old six-panelled door, covered in coal dust, and he took it home. Cleaned up, it was revealed to bear dozens of signatures—in fine, nineteenth-century script. Why A.D. Taylor and the Minnes boys, for example, would repeatedly sign the door, with date, remains a mystery. Was this some sort of warehouse door acting as logbook? The door featured an antique iron box lock, the key long gone, of course.

But when, one day, Sandy's nephews—both skilled carpenters who had done a lot of work on Sandy's log house—returned from Scotland with an ancient key found on the grounds of some abandoned castle (Castle Lachlan, in fact) and presented it to Sandy, he thought he would have the key retooled to make it fit.

One day, he's not sure why, he idly put the key inside the box and tried giving it a turn. With a reassuring click the lock accepted the key, and better, the key neatly turned the latch. Like Sandy MacLachlan and the things of the pioneers, the old black key from across the sea was a perfect fit.

wind

Betwixt wind and water is a nautical term describing "that part of the ship's side which is sometimes above water and sometimes submerged." In the days of cannon warfare, a shot that hit between wind and water was deemed especially dangerous. The cabin, most days, feels very much betwixt those two elements. Big water so close and beckoning, the big west wind coursing over the field and swirling through the cabin the second an open window affords entry.

In their book on the history of Prince Edward County, the writer Janet Lunn and her husband, Richard (a born-and-bred county lad now gone, sadly), observed that "because the county is flat and low," the wind is "an all-the-time wind. There's no getting away from the fact of its presence. The wind helped make the land, and the feel of it is everywhere." Janet was born in Vermont and now lives in Ottawa, but she says that living on the county's west coast for thirty-one years left her feeling a particular kinship with Holland, another small flat place defined by wind and water.

The wind is the county's life force. It stirs the trees, sets the high grass to whispering. Sends wave after wave to hammer county shores and herds the clouds above. Keeps my kite aloft and snapping like a snare drum. County wind has a rhythm: often slow to muster in the morning, liveliest in the afternoon, down for the count by dark. But the wind here is also unpredictable and full of mischief. It's the kind of wind that would remove a hat from a man's head and then send it rolling on its edge, like a tumbleweed, always out of reach of the pursuing hand. I've come back to the cabin from a swim to find the papers, receipts, and Post-it notes I left on the table in the southwest corner now banked against the east wall in the company of a dozen shanks of Dusty's blond fur. I've been up on scaffolding and ladders at the cabin and first lost my hat, and then my nerve, to the wind. The wind up there rises from below and billows my shirt, as if perturbed at finding something in its path. One day in the fall following a savage windstorm, I arrived at the cabin to find the north storm door wrenched from its hinges and lying on the grass, its glass impossibly intact. Proof of the wind's might and its sometimes coy mercy.

Still, I am glad of the wind at the cabin. The wind cools in summer, it braces year-round, and its constancy means that spring through fall when the trees are in leaf, there is almost always music in the air. The rustling sound is one I seem to need and I miss it terribly in winter, when the rustle becomes a howl. I sleep at the cabin by a west window, and when the wind is up it's almost like sleeping outside or in a tent. Sometimes I'll be sitting in the cabin's dead centre, and the *only* sounds I can hear are birdsong and the wind—now muffled like applause, now flexing its muscle, now filling the cabin with groans and whistles, as if someone were blowing in a bottle. It's the sound, I gather, of the wind squirrelling around inside the eavestroughs at the cabin's corners. In its texture and range and melody, the wind is very like the surf at the Point. They are county brothers, wind and water.

There exist a few river valleys in the county that wind often can't get to, but for the most part the county is a roofer's paradise where shingles are forever being sheared off houses. The county is a virtual island in Lake Ontario, set just west of where the lake narrows and flows into the St. Lawrence River. Shaped roughly like a diamond, and no more than thirty-one miles wide and eighteen and a half miles top to bottom, the county can claim a rugged and varied topography (the dunes at Sandbanks Provincial Park run up to eighty feet high), with several cliffs on the eastern flank and even a "mountain" or two. But by and large, the county hugs the ground, as if the land were hunkered against the west wind.

The county has been earmarked for a dozen or so huge wind turbines (almost forty storeys high) on its eastern coast. The gritty wind off the lake would generate what has come to be called green energy.

My feelings are mixed on this proposal. Questioning alternative energy is a bit like decrying the family farm, or saying you approve of something but not in my back yard. In summer 2001, I wrote a long feature on wind and solar power in *Canadian Geographic* magazine. Most readers of the piece would take from it the author's conviction that so-called green energy is a good thing, and the quicker we embrace it the better.

Why, then, am I troubled by the prospect of wind turbines coming to the county? The turbines would be close, just east of the Point. And until I read a report compiled by consultants hired by Vision Quest, the wind energy developer, I had underestimated how critical the Point is as a staging ground for migratory birds. The bird counts in that report are staggering and thrilling at the same time. What I take the report to say is that the Point is a pearl, one of North America's great ornithological resources. How great a resource is uncertain. How birds use the area, the report notes, is "poorly understood." At the same time, the report concedes that "birds move through the area in numbers far greater than those reported."

I wonder, then, why would one even contemplate locating a wind turbine farm in such close proximity to such a resource? What might be the impact of a great many turbines—by day, or by night if the turbines are lit or strobe-lit as has been suggested?

I also wonder about the wider impact on the county itself, which the county's official plan refers to in ideal terms, as "a tranquil and beautiful place to visit." Would wind turbines threaten that quiet? Where would the hydro lines and towers go to funnel that juice into the grid? I don't know, but I do know that one reason wind energy has not taken off is the noise of the machines. If you research the matter of wind turbines and noise, you will be struck by the assurances of low noise coming from turbine developers and the anecdotal evidence coming from those who live near such machines and who find the noise troublesome indeed. What might be the impact on the county soundscape of many dozens or perhaps hundreds of such machines? If one or two are approved, do we not pave the way for many more all over the county?

Finally, there is the matter of the turbines' height. While there are those who find wind turbines pleasing to look at, many would object. These turbines are four hundred feet high, this in a county where the highest buildings are two storeys high. The scale seems all wrong. Wind power's major drawbacks—too noisy, too ugly for some—have limited its residential use. Instead, it is large-scale, discreetly located wind farms that have some people chomping at the bit. Discreet this proposal is not; large-scale it may well become.

But I do know why the developer chose the county. The wind here is fierce. The Irish writer Flann O'Brien, in *The Third Policeman,* conjured the notion of each wind having its own particular colour, which the ancients would watch with pleasure. The vibrant west wind (amber, O'Brien says) is a blessing, for it forces blackflies and mosquitoes to shelter in the woods and not at the cabin. The wind also assails the aforementioned Point and some days gives it an oceanic swagger. On March 10, 2002, high winds racked Ontario, and the *Globe and Mail* reported that winds at the Point reached 135 kilometres (84 miles) an hour. The Point is one of the most windswept spots in the province, and thus its listing in a newspaper article comparing the windiest of wind-tossed locales. The Point juts far out into the lake, so winds from the west can gather speed as they race across more than one hundred miles of open water. We forget the power of wind to whip up a great lake: a lighthouse keeper on an island near Kingston reports finding fish 150 feet from the waterline. Flying fish.

Some years, Farmer Guernsey plants wheat in the ten-acre field where the cabin sits, and from the cabin's second storey I will watch the wind ripple and dart and play tag with kindred spirits. In high winds, the cabin is an old schooner on a yellow sea, and I am privileged by my view from the upper decks.

I would learn, though, that pioneers set their cabins in the woods in part because the trees offered a natural break against the wind. I will never forget coming to the cabin that first spring just after wind-driven rain had exposed all the flaws in the chinking. Buffetted by wind and water, the old schooner I had so lovingly restored was shown to leak badly; the entire south wall, you will recall, had to be rechinked. A cabin in an open field is no match for rain riding county winds. I was grateful to the elderly gentleman north of Toronto who confessed to me that his own square-timbered cabin leaked all right. "But I find it dries," he said with a smile. His aplomb assured me—for a while. Later I would read that wood constantly shifting between a wet and dry state is vulnerable to rot and bugs, and my brow began to furrow once more. Eventually, I put a water-repellent sealant on the chinking; that—and a porch on the south side—seemed finally to address the leaks.

Most weekends, and especially spring through fall, millions of Canadians migrate from the city to places in the country. Many people go to the cottage, which, though attractive in its own right, is often a different animal altogether from the cabin—that quieter, more removed, more meditative creature.

Let the following four cases make the point.

In a piece called "A Cabin in the Woods" (part of *Writing Home: A PEN Canada Anthology* published in 1997), the author and journalist Ron Graham describes what he was looking for when he began eyeing land in the Eastern Townships of Quebec. He wanted to be near friends on Lake Memphremagog and Lake Massawippi, he wanted fields, woods, a place to swim. And he wanted distance between himself and tourist towns, crowded beaches, loud motorboats, transmission lines, snowmobile trails, and traffic. "In truth," wrote Graham, "I was seeking nothing less than a spiritual refuge."

Just as William Thorsell did, Graham hung out occasionally over the course of several years at the ninety-acre piece of land he would eventually buy, using an old trailer as a base camp before finally building his one-room log cabin in the woods at the confluence of two rushing streams. Tucked into a valley, the cabin looks out on trees and sky, and the only sounds are of birds and that fast-flowing water. Graham writes, "I never feel so calm or free—so much at home—as I do [there] … When I was away, whether working in Toronto or travelling abroad, I drew comfort from the thought that there existed one speck of the globe, awaiting me like Ulysses' dog, permanently mine … a base from which I could go forth with a light step and to which I could return with a joyous heart."

For years, the Toronto novelist M.T. Kelly owned a simple A-frame on a small patch of near north land, a virtual island in the stream of two rivers. No hydro, no water, just a tiny bunkhouse and loft with a rough timber porch overlooking a clearing in the tall pines. It was his little Ponderosa, his sacred place.

The six-acre piece of sandy rock-strewn land came with an old aluminum fishing boat, a kind of ferry he would load with essentials—food and drink, propane for the Coleman stove, books and bedding, and an aging whippet named Pete. One hot summer day, I looked on as the powerfully built Kelly waded across the chest-deep river, leading the boat on a rope like St. Christopher. The cabin (*hermitage* more like it) was a five-minute portage farther on through the pines. Kelly has canoed whitewater rivers all over the country, including rivers in the High Arctic and some of the great rivers that flow into James Bay (David and I joined him on several of those memorable expeditions), and our joke is that age has laid us low, left us longing for soft wilderness: the dainty rivers that flow past Kel's cabin, the easy lift to the bunkhouse. (Not like that twice-covered three-mile portage on the Missinaibi.) Still, Kel needed a quiet place beyond the city, and his cabin—which looked like something Grey Owl would have built—filled that need for many years.

Monte Hummel, the Canadian conservationist and writer, wrote a book *(Wintergreen: Reflections from Loon Lake)* in praise of his own retreat in the woods and others like it. His place is a one-room cabin that lacks electricity, running water, and telephone, but in other ways it lacks for nothing. I imagine it to be a small jewel set on a tiny private lake surrounded by 270 acres of bush and rock in the Canadian Shield country northwest of Kingston.

Hummel talks about getting to know a place so well that the boundary between landscape and self begins to dissolve, and what comfort that brings. "Whatever this place may be," he writes, and here he's speaking generically about the special places that many of us know and cherish, "it's a safe harbour that makes no unwelcome demands. It serves as a source of sanity when everything else seems to be flying apart. It is not an escape from reality, but a return to what really counts and what counts as real."

Hummel goes to the cabin a few days every month, with longer visits in spring and fall. Much as I use my cabin, he typically goes there alone, though his family—his wife and two grown sons—often join him there. And, like me, he goes there to write. *Wintergreen* was penned there, sometimes by candlelight, and the quiet little book sketches the place through the seasons and the pure joy to be had there from birding, fishing and hiking, canoeing, stargazing, and quiet reflection. The cabin on Loon Lake is Hummel's "enduring sanctuary" and "spiritual well-spring" and his love for it shines through on every page.

The young Canadian blues guitarist Rick Fines tells me that he and his wife, Lise, years ago sought a getaway but had no interest in what he called "cottage culture." The then struggling musician approached his bank about a loan and was told they could borrow no more than eight thousand dollars. After privately cobbling together another four thousand dollars at the eleventh hour, they forked over twelve thousand dollars and took possession of a twelve-by-twelve-foot cedar cabin on thirty acres in the Haliburton Highlands about a hundred miles northeast of Toronto. It had the usual amenities: no phone, no electricity, no running water.

Fines tells of staying there for weeks while a frantic record producer, his pal Alec Fraser, tried to reach him. When the latter finally made contact, he accused Fines of "living the life of Riley." (I've heard Fines in concert tell the story about the actual nineteenth-century poet of means named James Whitcomb Riley who wrote romantic verse about the drudgeries of the poor.

According to one version of events handed down, the down-trodden did not take kindly to being patronized and accused him of "living the life of Riley." The expression lived on; the poet and his poetry have somewhat faded into obscurity.)

Out of that exchange with his producer came a Fines/Fraser song called "Riley Wants His Life Back" and a reminder that—for many of us—the life of Riley may mean a modest cabin or hunt camp in the woods, a tumbledown farmhouse bought as a summer place, or a trailer tucked away on a woodlot. To their owners, they are almost always more than they seem.

Graham, Kelly, Hummel, and Fines are artists, and artists are forever tipping us off to the existence of special places. I spoke with an art gallery owner in the county who moved here in 1986, when, he said, there were about thirty people who called themselves artists. Few made a living by their art, yet their art defined them. That will never change. But by 2003, the number of county people who called themselves artists—at least according to the gallery owner's count—had risen astronomically, to about 250. It was if they had blown in from Toronto and points east on the west wind, drawn by the light and the water, the island feel (and cheap rents), and the company of other painters.

Happy are they who love where they live. Few can make that claim.

Just days before Christmas, Ulrike and I traditionally go to a party at the home of friends in Yarker, a village close by the one we lived in for seventeen years. Margret Paudyn, whom we both know from our time in the country, was describing one year how she and her husband, Rick, are devoted to their secluded house and acreage on the Napanee River. "They'll take us away in pine boxes," she laughed.

"Sometimes," she said, "people love where they live and aren't aware of that powerful feeling for place." She recalled how years ago they had bought the property from an elderly man, grown feeble and sick. A week after the sale, he appeared in their driveway. He asked to come in and, at their kitchen table, tears streaming down his face, he spilled his deep regret, an anguish beyond assuaging. Every Saturday he would come, cry ritually at Margret's table, and ask permission to walk what was now their land, circle their pond, admire their trees. Within a year, he was dead, and his wife followed him shortly after that.

Why do some of us fall in love with land, even "flawed" land? What makes a place special? How can one be alone in a secluded place and not feel lonely there? My great-aunt Lizzie, who treasured her rocky swampy farmland north of Kingston, figures in my answer. As does the writer Matt Cohen, a neighbour of Lizzie's and a man who also dearly loved his land. Patsy Aldana, Matt's widow, told me that Matt used to honk his horn every time he crossed the county line en route to the four-hundred-acre farm north of Kingston he bought in 1970. "Matt really loved that land," she said, "because in the end he found peace there. He felt connected to it. It enabled him to cope with the world."

In *Typing*—the book he wrote as he was dying—Matt described how he could picture in his mind "every tiny corner of that farm, retrace every step of every walk that I took, remember the places where the snow lasted the longest … the hills with the best wild strawberries …" And yet later he describes how impossible it would have been for him to actually farm and work the land. His attachment to the land, he said, "was total, but my relationship was that of witness, observer and worshipper." Maybe not a bad thing, to worship the land. We've certainly had a go at defiling it.

My great-aunt Lizzie Foster and Matt Cohen were kindred spirits.

Lizzie was the sister of my grandfather, Leonard Flynn, who, with his wife, Gertrude (nee Dalton), farmed near Tamworth, a village northwest of Kingston. Leonard's father was born here, Leonard's grandfather in County Wicklow, Ireland, in 1830. But you would have been hard pressed to tell who was born in the old country and who was born here, so pronounced was the Irish accent through the generations. Near the Flynn farm was a village so Irish they called it Erinsville. Nanna, Grampa, and Lizzie, then, were all as Irish as potatoes, as Catholic as the pope, and all lived long—Lizzie longest of all.

Sometimes I shake my head in wonder at how much changed from the time they were all in their cradles to the time they were lowered into their graves. My grandmother was raised in the village of Douro, five or six miles from the log cabin homesteads of Susanna Moodie and Catharine Parr Traill. Little Gertrude Dalton, who would one day bear a daughter named Clare (who would, in turn, bear me), was eight years old when Traill died in 1899. In a way, the lives of the Traills and the Moodies and the Daltons all intersected, and knowing that Catharine and Susanna were literally neighbours of my grandmother's has deepened my feeling for them.

Only recently did it strike me that the Moodie and Traill cabins were within paddling distance of our old family cottage. Had I taken a notion, I could have canoed west from our old place on Lower Buckhorn Lake, portaged around Burleigh Falls, and paddled south on Stony Lake and on into Lake Katchawanooka to the Traills' precious cabin, which they called Westove—after the family homestead in the Orkneys. Of all the cabins and cottages the Moodies and Traills ever lived in, only Westove and a stone cottage in Belleville have survived.

Westove, which mightily impressed Susanna when she first saw it, featured on the ground floor a kitchen, a large parlour with a bedroom that led from it, a pantry, and a storage closet—all heated by a Franklin stove. On the walls of the parlour hung maps and prints and over the windows were curtains of green linen and white muslin. There was a noticeable warmth about the cabin, with the smell of baking often pervading the place and Catharine's fine patchwork quilts adding splashes of brightness and colour. An open staircase led upstairs, which would later be divided into three bedrooms, and below the cabin was a cellar for storing vegetables through the winter.

Though the rooms were dark owing to the tiny windows, Westove boasted two splendid refinements: a small pane of glass in the parlour window that afforded a view of Lake Katchawanooka, and the cabin's perch on a little peninsula (which Catharine called "the Point") that caught breezes on humid summer days. Susanna's squared-cedar-log house, a mile to the north, would be bigger than her sister's. She called it "a palace" compared to "the miserable hut" they sheltered in during their first (and notably severe) winter in Canada in 1832.

Catharine, Susanna, Gertrude, Lizzie: these women had a hard go of it and I am astonished that they lived as long as they did. But none lived longer than Lizzie, who died in 1994 at the age of 100 and just a month shy of her 101st birthday.

"I'm going to Schmo," Grampa would say, or he would begin one of his long rambling tales, "I mind the time at Schmo ..." I thought Schmo a strange name, and my spelling was just a guess, for I had never seen it written. But for most of my life I thought Schmo was a real place, as real as Chippewa and Cedar Hill, other places my grandfather often talked about. Only recently did I come to realize that these places exist on no map. Why would Grampa say he was going to "Schmo" and not "Lizzie's place"? Then it hit me; when I talk about going to my folks' house in Scarborough, or my in-law's place in Toronto, I say I'm going to Sherwood Avenue or Kendal Avenue. The geographic code is the same.

I went to Schmo many times as a boy in the 1950s. When Lizzie Flynn married Jim Foster, a quiet steady man, she found herself at the helm of a large homestead that included Jim, his sister, and their mother—both women, my mother once told me, as sweet as angels. But Lizzie's new mother-in-law was severely crippled by arthritis and it fell to Lizzie to care for her, then for her own son, Joe, when he came, to milk the cows, weed the garden, help run the farm at Schmo, back of the village of Verona ...

It wasn't much of a farm—all rock and beaver pond, red and white cedar. Joe, when he was old enough, drove a truck on a milk route; that's how they survived. Joe had one withered hand, the result of a childhood blood infection passed on from his mother, who endured a lifetime of guilt.

Many people in Lizzie's circumstances would have been bitter, but she was not. Even those who didn't much like her had to admire her spirit. "I'm here," she would say of her lot in life, "and I'll make the best of it." Lizzie was plucky, and lucky too. She was partnered with a good man and, as poor as the farm was, as thin as the soil was, she loved Schmo. She was Schmitten.

Electricity came, then the telephone, and Nanna would sometimes ring up Lizzie on the party line (the one my cousins and I loved to eavesdrop on until an operator gave us a severe scolding one day and we were cured of our indiscretion). "How's the weather over there?" Nanna might ask, as a courtesy, for Schmo was only about ten miles away and the weather was surely the same. The curious thing was this: Lizzie always insisted that Schmo's weather was just fine, certainly better than Tamworth's. It might be grey and raining in Tamworth, but the sun was always shining in Schmo.

I have a vivid memory of Lizzie Foster with a switch in her hand, standing out by the swinging farm gate, tapping the switch firmly into the palm of her other hand and threatening to use it if we got out of line that day. I was sitting on the gate with my cousin Paul. We were perhaps ten and eleven. Even then I saw her as a tough old bird, face like a hawk. Lizzie was as sharp and acerbic as my grandfather was patient and warm. But there must have been a twinkle in Lizzie's eye that day; I don't remember fear. I see now that she was flirting with us. "Lizzie loved the boys," my mother would say. Unusual for her time, the tall and imposing Lizzie liked the company of men for she thought herself at least their equal.

Lizzie was my mother's godmother, but not the fairy kind. Whenever Nanna had a baby (she had four, all at home, and lost many others through miscarriage), Lizzie would go to Tamworth and help around the farm while Nanna nursed her infant and got back on her feet. My mother and her siblings, used to their ever kind mother, were taken aback by what they took to be Lizzie's tyranny. But she was a natural for the job, since she and my grandfather were great friends (though later they would sour on each other). My mother's great fear as a child was that her parents would die by some terrible circumstance and she would be forced to live with Lizzie.

Jim Foster died. Joe Foster died. Lizzie Foster lived on. She stayed in Schmo until the mid-1980s before moving into Providence Manor in Kingston, where she continued to display her viceregal manners. Even the nuns who ran the old folks' home gave her a wide berth. On weekends, she coerced the staff to bring her lunch up to her room. Not for *her* the company of the aged and confused rabble. Once when I went to see her, Lizzie dispatched her own roommate, who was sitting peaceably on her bed, so Lizzie and I could have "a proper visit." The woman fled as if chased by bees.

I liked Lizzie, in part because she liked me. I gave as good as I got from her, and she respected that. I sorely missed my grandfather after he died and Lizzie let me still connect with him in some way, for she had his wit, the same strong hands, the same sense of ease with the world and absolute certainty of her place in it.

Now Matt. A few days after Matt died, some of his writer friends—Wayne Grady, Merilyn Simonds, Diane Schoemperlen, Joan Finnigan, Ginny Moss—all gathered at a Kingston restaurant we call The Pig, though Chez Piggy is its proper name.

That day, a grand pile of Matt's books fully occupied one seat, with his photo on top, and we shared Cohen lore over drinks. I had no idea he was such a gifted tennis player, and I laughed at the story of Matt meddling on Merilyn's behalf: hoping to cause trouble and right a wrong, he dragged Merilyn to the office of a certain publisher who owed her a sizeable sum.

There were other revelations that day. At one point I was talking to Wayne about the obituary in the *Kingston Whig-Standard* and its mention of Schmo. For Matt's beloved cabin was just down from Lizzie's place on the Schmo Road. Wayne scoffed at the newspaper reporter who had misspelled Schmo when he mentioned in his article Matt's joke about living in Schmoville.

"What do you mean?" I asked.

"It's spelled *Chameau,*" Wayne said, wondering (and not for the first time) at my stupidity. "Matt used to joke all the time that he was the mayor of Chameauville." Matt had told Wayne that, according to local lore, someone had raised camels near his place a long time ago. Those camel farmers were perhaps French, since the French word for camel is *chameau;* ergo the Chameau Road. None of this would have been lost on Matt, a gifted translator of Québécois literature. Matt also mused, and typically, that they called the place *chameau* because the land was so very lumpy.

It took days for all this to sink in. On my map of the world, Schmo was suddenly gone and in its stead stood Chameau.

I wondered if Matt ever met Lizzie, in the general store at Bellrock, at the post office in Verona. Surely he would have heard stories about her. Maybe Lizzie or someone like her crept into one of his Salem novels, the triptych set in the hard country north of Kingston. And I wondered, too, what Lizzie would have made of him. Lizzie, who had little schooling, would not have been cowed by Matt's education and command of language. Matt could be blunt; so could Lizzie. They would have shared a sense of mischief.

My own contact with Matt was limited, more professional than personal. For eight years in the 1980s, I was book editor at the *Whig-Standard* and interviewed Matt several times, after he had written a novel or in connection with his work at the Writers' Union. After he wrote *The Spanish Doctor* (the "uncorrected advance proof" remains on my bookshelf), I must have made some comment—either in our conversation or the subsequent newspaper article—about the geriatric sex in the novel. In a letter by way of reply, Matt turned my comment on its side. He said he had taken note of my special interest and would endeavour to incorporate more of same in future works.

I also saw Matt socially. Every summer, for example, Wayne Grady would mark his own birthday with a baseball game in Kingston, and friends—Matt always included—would play nine innings, then gather at Wayne and Merilyn's house for food and drink.

Matt's death, and its effect on me, took me by slow surprise. I liken the process to discovering that you're somehow related to a dead man and want to learn more about him—especially when you find that one of your passions in life was also his. The first shock of discovery is followed by others, and they hit like waves.

I heard Dennis Lee on CBC Radio talk about walking Matt's land with him decades ago, sitting in a ramshackle outbuilding, the two of them watching the smoke from Dennis's pipe waft up to the hole in the roof, but only after passing through a diagonal shaft of light. It was an arresting image, two friends at peace in the quiet of their company. The image spoke of Matt's pure contentment on that land, which puzzled Dennis, for he saw Matt as quintessentially urban.

The picture that Dennis drew on the radio that day meshed with my linking of Schmo and Chameau, of Lizzie and Matt. But like Dennis, I was still trying to understand the source of Matt's affection for that land and cabin. And I put the question to Patsy Aldana.

Matt, she told me, was born in Kingston, and he must have felt a sense of homecoming each time he came back to the region of his birth. The land was his safe haven and he was as happy there alone as he was with Patsy and the kids. Told of Lizzie's penchant for exaggerating the quality of weather at Chameau, Patsy said that Matt would have had his own perverse take on that: "He would have said the sun *never* shines in Chameau."

Matt and Patsy fought about that land a lot, for he wanted desperately to live there year-round with his family. But this was impossible for all kinds of practical reasons. And maybe Matt came to realize, as I did, that were the refuge to become permanent residence, it would lose some of its magic. Contempt would follow familiarity, Ulrike warned me, and we would weary of playing pioneer. With no city to retreat from, my whole notion of retreat would come unravelled.

As Matt was dying, he worried about that land, about the trees, for he had watched them grow. Who would admire them when he was gone? Matt feared that Patsy would be forced to sell the land, and she assured him that she never would. Matt's children cherish that place and going there is a way of being with their father again, for some of his ashes, Patsy told me, are buried at Chameau.

Learning all this left me with a new and powerful feeling for Matt. Unbeknownst to me, he had what I have: an intimate feeling for a small piece of land so removed as to assure quiet or only the sounds that nature makes. And, as Matt was, I am as happy at the cabin alone as with family and friends for company. Like Patsy, Ulrike does not share my deep feeling for the place, and it's been (though more in the past than now) a source of contention. I take great pleasure there in small things: the crazy, darting ripple of the wind through the field of wheat that surrounds the cabin, how the fields transform themselves every day simply because the quality of light is so markedly different at dawn and at dusk (a painter friend assures me that this is no mere illusion, that the light in that area has no counterpart in the city). At night, the starry skies and coyotes' call renew, unfailingly, my sense of wonder. It seems I breathe more deeply there, as perhaps Matt did at his refuge.

There was even, in the story of Matt's refuge, a log cabin connection, and that, too, only revealed itself by and by. Among Matt's neighbours and friends around Bellrock—at least in the early days—were other writers and artists: Michael Ondaatje, Kim Ondaatje, John Moss, Ginny Moss. The Mosses had breathed new life into old logs after spotting a tumbledown cabin near Croydon, the remnants of a village fourteen miles from Bellrock. I knew Croydon, for my grandmother's twin sister, Loretta Murphy, had lived with her family at Croydon.

In his book *Bellrock,* published in 1983, John Moss describes buying what remained of a squared-cedar-log house from a Mr.

South in Croydon for the sum of one hundred dollars and, after a pretense at haggling, they got their log shell—"crumbling, roofless, dessicated, behind a pall of renegade lilacs, the ghosts not gone, but settled, merged with the wasting remains." The Mosses numbered the beams, carted them away, and floated them to a small island they had purchased at the village of Bellrock on the Depot Creek branch of the Napanee River. They were years—hard years full of joys and setbacks, rage and despair and jubilation—making those old logs into a home, but home they did become. It seemed to matter that the old logs had had other tenants in another century, and one year an older woman came by and out of curiosity asked for a tour of the place. Perhaps a cousin of old Mr. South, she pointed to one corner of the cabin which, she said, marked both his entry to this world and his exit: where his cradle had sat and where his body was laid out for the wake. Mr. South was just one of the log house's "ghosts not gone, but settled." John Moss named the cabin Bellrock, clearly prized it, and called it "our form of survival."

As for Matt's bush and rock, it was bush and rock that both he and my great-aunt Lizzie loved to their deaths. If Matt Cohen was the mayor of Chameauville, then Lizzie Foster was its queen mother. And if they never made each other's acquaintance while breathing, I hope they have by now.

I wish that county winds would drive away what passes for a scourge at the cabin, one that most who live in the country know well: the cluster fly. Not just one, either, but thousands. Some city people love to hear stories such as the one I am about to tell, for it hardens and sustains their conviction that they should stay right where they are.

A little entomology is in order here. The cluster fly looks very like the housefly, but where houseflies are solo fliers, the cluster fly gathers in … clusters, mathematical clusters. On sunny fall days I see them basking on the side of the cabin—on the east to catch the morning sun, then the south for the afternoon sun, and finally on the west side to catch the last rays. But they're not basking; they're thinking. Where shall we hunker down for the winter, lads? What about this old place, with all the inviting cracks? Sounds like a plan, they say, and find their way in.

One summer was particularly wet, and the cluster flies entered the cabin like so many unwelcome guests. I hung two sticky flypaper rolls from every window and, within a week, the brown of the rolls was completely masked by the black of the flies. So many raisins on a glistening ribbon of glue. I learned that cluster flies lay their eggs on earthworms, and rain that summer had brought up the worms, which became hosts to all those flies, whose offspring were now stuck to the flytraps. By their buzzing, they seemed none too pleased, but neither was I. At night, I would sit in my rocker and read by the light of a goose-necked lamp (a five-dollar gem found in a second-hand store in Kingston), but the flies were drawn to the light and made reading a chore. Like manic asteroids in orbit around a small sun, they would ping off my face, my book, the bulb. Every turned-on light in the cabin drew new orbiters, and so to the beams by every naked bulb I tacked glue traps. They glistened like so much brown tinsel. Caught flies buzzed angrily. Over time, the resin would lose its tackiness and the corpses would drop like fetid rain. What is a man to do when his hard-won sanctuary is sullied with damn gnats?

The man becomes obsessed. I'd vacuum forty and fifty at a time from each window in the cabin, but by the time I was at the last window—number eleven—the first window had forty new tenants. Their droppings peppered the glass, their buzzing grated day and night, and the bodies of the dead were staining the pine window sills I had so lovingly oiled and varnished (I would eventually come to lay cedar roofing shingles over each sill every fall, just as some people lay protective tarps over treasured cars to spare them from winter's ravages). I even imagined I could smell the flies, a slightly rancid smell like a bruise on fruit.

My war on the flies would, the following year, become both defensive and offensive. I was like Leningen, the hero of a short story I had read as a boy, and, like Leningen, who waged methodical and multi-frontal war on the army ants that laid siege to his home in the jungle, I gave more time and energy to the cluster fly war than I care to admit. I discovered that the south door (a nineteenth-century retread bought from Connor) had sagged with time, and that up in the corner where it met the door frame was a yawning quarter-inch gap that only started to narrow as it should halfway across the width of the door. For cluster flies, this was a highway, one anyway, to heaven. By some ad hoc weather-stripping, I shut down that ramp. Then—surmising that the flies were getting past the screens and from there into labryinthine spaces at the windows—I decided to leave the screens on all fall, with weatherstrip tape (actually clear hockey tape) all around them to shut off that access as well.

I also bought, on the advice of a friend, something called a Cluster Buster. The thing works on the knowledge that cluster flies seek small spaces to enter and overwinter. This trap features just such an entryway at the top, but inside the pocket—about the size of a hockey elbow pad and about as elegant—is a white dust made from finely crushed egg shells. Organic gardeners use something similar, called diatomaceous earth, in the garden: the lethal dust—made from the silica shells of prehistoric algae—scores the bodies of insects tracking overtop, and they eventually die of dehydration. I liked the theory of the Cluster Buster; in practice, the one trap I deployed experimentally adhered badly to the window, and when the trap falls off, as mine did several times, its fine white dust floats in the air for hours and drifts to every part of the cabin, enters the nose, and hangs in the air like a crystalline fog. The cure posed almost more nuisance than the ailment.

Some people take a more aggressive approach. They buy a Vapona No-Pest Strip—a slow-release insecticide that is hell on bugs, and surely on humans too—and hang it in the attic where the flies think they have found a secure winter bunk, a base for their forays into the rooms below. And there's always the option of calling in the pesticide people, who will spray exterior walls with their own version of entomological napalm. But every year you'll have to call in another air strike, and every air strike, I'll wager, exacts a price.

In keeping with the way I run the place, I'm sticking with incessant vacuuming, maniacal weatherstripping, and the same gooey flytraps my grandparents used at the farm—and that apparently terrified me as a child.

One fall, flummoxed by the way one window—the one at the top of the stairs—was drawing flies in truly exorbitant numbers, I simply waited and watched, trying to spot the source of this flow of traffic. Eventually the gateway revealed itself: where the window sits on the highest log, there are small caverns where either the foam insulation or caulking wasn't applied, or perhaps the settling of the logs had created new openings. In any case, I applied clear tape over these spots to see if it might curtail entry. Within a minute, there were a dozen flies running up and down the horizontal spaces behind the tape. "Que pasa!" they were saying. "This road was free and clear yesterday, what's up?"

I would get out the foam canisters and the caulking gun, I would buy fly-glue traps by the six-pack. But every fall it is the same, now more, now less. On quiet calm days, the buzzing of cluster flies is as loud inside the cabin as it is outside, louder still inside my head. And I think, Susanna Moodie must have had cluster flies, too. Maybe it was the flies—one scourge too many—that finally soured her on life in the colonies.

Even in late October, when the cold sees the flies tucked away in their winter beds, the act of firing up the woodstove or turning on lights at night draws some out again. "Yo boys," they tell one another, "must be summer!" I am, as I write this, fashioning in my mind a kind of box kite made of strands of fly glue set at right angles to one another. It would hang so that the bare bulb in the ceiling would form its brilliant centre, to which the critters would be drawn. I would flick on that one light, take Dusty for a long walk and return to find every fly in the place caught in my luminous snare.

If, one day, I envelop my entire pioneer cabin in fly screen or muslin—like some oversized malarial tent—you will know that cluster flies finally put me over the edge.

Not all bugs that ride in on the west wind are so troublesome. For most of one September, the ten-acre field that surrounds the cabin—where Farmer Guernsey had that year sewn clover and hay—was home to thousands of yellow butterflies. They would rest in the morning in the shade of the hedgerow, but in the sun never cease to flutter, seemingly charged by the light. The effect was almost dainty, myriad yellow baubles dancing, as if pieces of the sun had dropped to earth or a giant had hung shimmering pennies on invisible string for the pleasure of seeing them spin in the wind.

At dusk, the butterflies would settle, exhausted by their endeavours. All day they had circled, risen, and fallen, yet they were not so focused on their work that you could get near them. After the sun dropped, though, they were easily captured. Only then did I see that the butterflies were double winged, the outer pair yellow, the inner a lime green. The outer wings featured two dots, one black, one white, splendid little moons with other dots—I took them for asteroids—in their shadow. After a day of manic vacuuming of cluster flies, I was grateful to behold such beauty.

In the grass closer to the cabin, another insect lay waiting for its meals to arrive. I'm not sure why, but the cabin has drawn dozens of praying mantises, those imperious hunters. As David and I worked on the pergola, every twenty minutes I would have to lift one off a beam we were about to raise high and set the long fellow in the high grass nearby. As an experiment, I even brought one into the cabin and parked him at the window at the top of the stairs—the cluster fly capital of the world. If the mantis couldn't devour them all, maybe word of his presence would spread on the cluster fly internet. Alas, the mantis seemed as dumbfounded as I was by all the buzzing. He ate not a one and the flies ignored him. I returned him to his proper domain.

The lanky creatures hunker down in the grass with their great grasping limbs set to clamp down on passing grasshoppers or crickets. The females I saw were brown, the colour of an oak leaf in the fall, and their abdomens were swollen with eggs. I like to think that keeping the field organic accounts, in part, for the profusion of these rulers of the lower world. The word *mantis* is from the Greek and it means diviner or prophet; in France, according to legend, a praying mantis would point a lost child home.

Summer 2002. Languid heat. The least movement, any exertion, causes sweat to form on my forehead. My Irish thermostat wasn't built for this. On such days, the cabin is bereft—*I* am bereft—of breezes. The animals, the birds know to stay still in such crippling heat. Leaves on trees barely stir, as if they, too, know the folly of motion. A plane droning in the distance, the low hum of Oma's fridge are the only sounds I can decipher.

But the county winds soon resurrect themselves. Stiff breezes make the thirty-degree heat—in the shade of trees anyway—

bearable. A temperature gauge in the cabin tells me, one day near the end of July, that it's twenty-eight degrees inside, but the breezes make it comfortable. One need only don shorts, open the windows wide, and let the west wind work its magic.

The same wind that provoked three-foot-high breakers at the shore and that cowed my pup has raced over fields and trees, past the grazing cows and men on their riding lawnmowers, past the resplendent country properties and the white-trash gardens of rusted metal, past the blue tree house I admire on my way to the Point, on and on to me.

One fall day I rode my sturdy young Canadian horse in the outdoor ring at the stable north of Kingston where he resides. The wind was howling that morning, the leaves were whirling like dervishes, and somewhere a door kept opening and slamming, opening and slamming. I thought about cancelling the ride altogether, or riding inside. High winds can unnerve a horse, for the roar robs him of the acute hearing he uses to foretell danger. He thus feels more vulnerable and is more apt to spook and run, and, in the process, ditch the rider. What rider? he says. The horse is a flight animal.

I thought of that ride some weeks later when I was walking in our woods with Dusty and saw two massive beech trees snapped off at the six-foot mark. Where once stood proud trees there were now two jagged monuments, sharp angry spears of cream-yellow wood. The trees were still attached to their trunks but only by the slimmest of umbilical chords. The beeches' crime was to be tall and thus in the maw of the same wind—or, rather, its wilder county cousin—that had panicked Dali and saw him go face first into the cedar hedge that lines one side of the outdoor ring. I had laughed at this, cantered him several rounds to make a point, then called it a day. Wind had sent me packing.

In the forest, a tree will often come down in its entirety, the root ball up in the air and exposed like a grandmother's knickers. After windstorms I make a point of inspecting our forest, counting the fallen—sometimes a dozen strong. I am often astonished by how gingerly, how desperately, did a massive tree grip the earth. Hardly more than knuckle deep. My hunch, though, was that the beeches were dug in, and that the soil is deep on that rare piece of high ground where a beech grove flourishes. The beeches' great girth and roots likely spared them the indignity of being uprooted but weren't enough to let them face down the county wind.

Both beeches had fallen in the same direction, to the west, so the wind was a rare easterly. The fenceline, gnarled cedar lengths set on triangular supports of the same wood, had snapped where the beeches had fallen. It saddened me to see the most imposing of the two beeches go down, for this was likely the thickest tree in the woods. It would have taken two of me to encircle it with my/our arms. The bark was grey and smooth, like skin, not like the rough diamond shapes of the ash, or the Braille-like notchings of the poplar, or thorned like the locust, or broken like the shagbark hickory. The beech is a tree you want to touch, and I had touched this tree often on our walks and looked up admiringly into its canopy—the same great spread that now lay on the ground.

In the cabin's early days, I had asked the excavator to truck the rock turned up during the creation of the basement to a spot at the southwest corner of the forest. My own rocky entryway, one inspired by experience of mud.

I had managed, foolishly, to get my truck mired down there in spring during tree planting. Another year I got the truck stuck in the middle field—again during spring tree planting. "Aren't you worried about getting stuck?" inquired a lad we had hired in the village to help. He was twelve, and it was his observation that the truck tires were beginning to sink into the mire. We were all in sou'westers and rain gear against the downpour. "Nah, it'll be fine," I assured him and we went back to planting. Later that day a neighbour came over with his tractor and extracted the truck with a smile and a tsk.

To be stuck a second time near the forest was quite fitting: royal punishment for royal stupidity. That business still fresh in my mind, I had the excavator use the disinterred stone to make a small road a few feet above the wet ground. I had thought it would allow me to back the truck right to the edge of the forest for firewood gathering. But I've never mustered the nerve to use that little stone road, now thick with sumac and tall weeds. Even when the ground is frozen, the mud long gone, I can't bring myself to drive past an imaginary line I have drawn east to west across that field. I am like sailors in the time of the explorers who thought the world was flat and feared falling over the edge.

Sometimes the night wind will bring with it the whiff of skunk, though our place in the city is a more likely draw. (I chatted with a friend on our porch one summer night and counted six skunks in my range of vision; garbage night is always a good time to view urban wildlife.)

Dusty has been sprayed by skunks several times—at both house and cabin. I keep tomato juice on hand after that first encounter at the cabin. Near midnight I had stepped outside to admire the stars when Dusty heard something in the field, set her shoulders, and bounded off. It must have been March, for snow was still gathered where winds converge at the southeast corner of the cabin, and when she returned a minute later she began frantically to roll her head and neck in that snow in a sad and feeble attempt to throw off the bracing reek. The effect of the foul-smelling secretion, called mercaptan and produced in the skunk's anal glands, is nothing like the odour that provokes mild wrinkling of the nose when your car passes over old roadkill. The freshly delivered stuff—which can be sprayed at a range of up to thirteen feet—is primal and overpowering. If I, with my poor human nose—one already dulled with age—cannot bear it, imagine the plight of the poor pup with her heightened olfactory senses. Despite repeated baths in tomato juice, countless shampoos, and the steady work of ultraviolet light, six months after the incident a little rain still manages to freshen the musky scent and recall the memory of that striped member of the weasel clan.

One afternoon at the cabin, David was backing out his van after a visit when Dusty spotted a skunk at the end of the driveway. She took off in a flat-out gallop but, bless her, came back when I called her. *Call,* though, falls short of capturing my repeated shrieking of her name. Whether she's learned about skunks after three encounters or was responding to my hysteria is hard to say. She doesn't always heed my call when nature beckons.

Another time, while walking along the road that fronts the cabin, we flushed what looked to be a miniature deer (it was more likely a very young one) from cover in the bush, and Dusty chased that delicate bounding creature through three fields, the gap between them widening with each field, before she finally gave up the pursuit. My last sight of the deer was of it leaping in the high grass in Dick and Anne's field south of our land, now arcing over the grass, now disappearing into it like a gazelle on springs or a dolphin flashing in and out of water. I had worried for the deer's fate, but by the end of the chase I think the pursued was toying with her pursuer. As the *Racing Form* sometimes says of horses that finish well back, Dusty was outrun, spent, had no late rally, no late bid, she was up the track. She came back with her tongue hanging out though evidently well pleased with the adventure.

Nights at the cabin I wrestle with what menaces her in the dark. If the coyotes seem too close for comfort, I might keep her in, for I've read too many stories of the clever coyote enticing lone dogs with promises of play or romance before an unseen second coyote dashes in to tilt the odds and a family pet is done like dinner. If I've seen porcupines or raccoons around or smell skunk, Dusty stays inside. But she enjoys the night air as much as I do, and I give her her freedom more often than not.

Her worst ordeal occurred at the cabin, and her attackers numbered in the millions. Dusty, the vet later surmised, must have rolled in the carcass of some dead creature—maybe a squirrel—infected with mange, read ear mites. Dogs love to roll in rotted fish or stinking matted fur, the stinkier the better. It's a holdover from the days when their ancestors hunted and sought to mask their scent from prey. I began to notice black crust forming at the edges of Dusty's floppy, pointed ears and thought little of it, but a day or so later—while swimming at the Point—I observed that her nose was also glistening red and swollen, as if hornets had stung her there and ripped off flesh for good measure.

Dusty seemed agitated, was scratching her ears, and the lesion on her nose seemed to be growing before my eyes. We hustled her to the vet in town. For weeks, we gave her medication, applied alcohol to her scabs and wounds, and watched as the itching—and the licking of paws, the shaking of the head, and other signs of misery—only slowly subsided. Henceforth, Dusty would get prophylactic medication against the mites.

The stealth and resourcefulness of parasites is remarkable. I travelled as a young man in Morocco and camped on a beach with other wanderers, among them a crew of Aussies who had served in Vietnam and who knew about ticks. One of the creatures had made his own camp in my chest, just below my chin and line of vision. The Aussie applied a just-burnt match to my skin and when the tick stuck its head out, my friend used a safety pin to grab it by the head and pry it out. I was appalled and amazed to see the tick, engorged with my blood, thus evicted.

Another time, while living in the village of Camden East, I took our cat Monica Clare to the vet when a sore on her head would not heal. The vet, immediately wise to the problem, applied alcohol to the festering wound and when a grub peeked out, it was similarly seized upon with tweezers and extracted. I was astonished by its dimensions—almost the size of my thumb. The parasitic worm, or rather the egg that would give shape to it, had apparently been waiting in the grass for likely accommodation, and our young feline was it. The cat had snacked on something overtop the grass, ingested the egg, and the creature had hatched inside Monica Clare's stomach and grown before migrating to new digs in her skull.

A friend of mine, a biologist who has done work in Central America, wrote amusingly of a similar experience—that of a colleague in whom a parasite had migrated to a spot on the top of his head. Imagine a lump the size of a golf ball perched on a human scalp and become the object of many inquiries, the cause of many gasps. He eventually had it removed, though not without some regret, for he had grown … attached to the thing.

Dusty and I have yet to be rained down upon by wood ticks, though this, too, may come with the territory of the cabin and its forested land. In Canada there are thirty-five species of the order of ticks known as Acari and some ten thousand species of mites, members of the same order. Theirs is a world we know little of; only 20 per cent of mites in this country have been scientifically described and catalogued, but there is no denying their numbers. One square yard of forest soil may contain one million mites, representing a hundred species. For the most part, they seem to go their way, and Dusty and I go ours.

Man going one way, nature the other. That's pretty much the way it was for much of recorded history. (At least in Western culture; Eastern religions—Buddhism, Hinduism, Shinto—revered nature and urged compassion for all living things.) There did exist this notion in early Christianity of the wilderness as a place where sinners went to be purified, to meditate and pray (think of St.

Anthony and all the hermits who sought the solitude of the desert), but the more prevailing opinion held that the wilderness was evil. Christian missionaries took as their first task to cut down the sacred groves where pagans had worshipped. The forest prime evil.

Small wonder that when the pioneers arrived in North America, wilderness was seen as even more forbidding than the increasingly tame version then available in Europe. In the New World, if the wolves and cougars didn't get you, the Indians would. To be lost in the woods meant certain death. The menace of the woods would slowly give way to the romance of the woods, with the pens of Thoreau and Emerson leading the way in the middle of the nineteenth century. But only a few decades before that, the woods were still a scary place for the frontiersman.

When, in 1831, Alexis de Tocqueville made his celebrated trip to the United States and informed his hosts of his wish to see the wilderness—for it was novel to him and he thought the experience would be a pleasureable one—the locals in Michigan thought he was crackers. In his *Democracy in America,* de Tocqueville came to the conclusion that while Europeans talk a great deal about the wilds of North America, Americans themselves "never think about them; they are insensible to the wonders of inanimate nature and they may be said not to perceive the mighty forests that surround them till they [the forests, that is] fall beneath the hatchet." They have other notions, de Tocqueville said: "draining swamps, turning the course of rivers, peopling solitudes, and subduing nature." The only good tree, in other words, was a downed tree.

But self-preservation was not the only force at work here. Contempt for nature and any who embraced nature marked first contact between Christopher Columbus and the indigenous people of the Caribbean, just as it would later define relations in New England between the Pilgrims and First Peoples. Trading would begin in genteel fashion, but any theft on the part of the incumbents was met with swift and extreme retribution. The death of a Christian inevitably warranted a response that tilted toward the genocidal.

All this still matters, some five hundred years later, because such a span in human history is no span at all. Call it the life spans of five humans who lived to a ripe old age.

Why do some of us, many of us, feel so disconnected from the land and from nature? Why does the thought of a cabin in the woods feel so alluring to some, so foreign and even alien to others? Some historians argue that the answers lie with Columbus and the Pilgrims. In a classic book called *Beyond Geography: The Western Spirit Against the Wilderness,* first published in 1980 and still enjoying wide readership, the American author Frederick Turner argues that both the conquistadores and the Pilgrims strutted under a Christian banner that led them to believe they were better than the Godless naked heathens. And if the natives were given to respect wilderness and all living things, then this, too, was suspect. When the Spanish, writes Turner, "did take note of the native presence, it was with the curled lip of disgust." Columbus's first thoughts were of how to exploit this new land. Find the gold and bring it home. Fill the holds of ships with slaves. Convert the soulless natives in quick order.

If the natives felt a powerful connection with the earth, it did not move the Spanish or the Pilgrims to emulate them or to rethink their biblically ordained position (the Book of Genesis set out that man would have *dominion* "over the fishes of the sea, and the fowls of the air, and the beasts, and the whole earth, and every creeping creature that moveth upon the earth"). On the contrary.

When Hernando Cortés encountered natives in 1519 and observed the gold they wore, he bade them bring him some, for, as he told them, "I and my companions suffer from a disease of the heart which can only be cured with gold." Turner notes the dark truth in that remark and goes on to argue that if the Europeans who came to the New World rarely felt a sense of place or kinship with this new land, this is in large part because that land was simply seen as a commodity. Like gold and spices, lumber and buffalo and cod.

Most pioneers, Turner believes, did not see themselves as permanent settlers, but as potential realtors, flipping land and moving on, as Daniel Boone used to do. We see the result today—what Turner calls a "profound estrangement of the inhabitants from their habitat: a rootless, restless people with a culture of superhighways precluding rest and a furious penchant for tearing up last year's improvements in a ceaseless search for some gaudy ultimate." Ouch.

Turner is not alone. As Roderick Nash points out in *Wilderness and the American Mind*—a lively book that chronicles the evolution of environmentalism—"appreciation of wilderness began in the cities. The literary gentleman wielding a pen, not the pioneer with his axe, made the first gestures of resistance against the strong currents of antipathy." And Nash tells, to illustrate, the remarkable story of Estwick Evans.

He was a lawyer in New Hampshire who made an extraordinary four-thousand-mile trek west in 1818—in winter, the better to experience "the pleasure of suffering and the novelty of danger." Evans did it in style, donning a buffalo robe trimmed with bearskin and with two dogs for company. He wrote about the experience, of course, and had much good to say about the advantages of solitude and the pure silence of nature. "There is something in the very name of wilderness," he wrote, "which charms the ear, and soothes the spirit of man. There is religion in it."

In his learned and wide-ranging book *Landscape and Memory,* the historian Simon Schama takes a completely different tack from that of Turner and Nash. Schama would argue that our connection with nature is bred in the bone and derives from ancient religious traditions. As he observes, "the cultural habits of humanity have always made room for the sacredness of nature." The Christians, says Schama, "hijacked" pagan myths rooted in landscape and memory, so when "we scramble the slopes or ramble the woods, our Western sensibilities carry a bulging backpack of myth and recollection." If I feel a sense of the divine in the fields and forests around the cabin, Schama would say that it has everything to do with my Catholic and Celtic past. If I bring to *my* sacred place all manner of religious sentiment, I am in good company. Nordic tree worship, Christianity's Tree of Life, pagan groves, cathedral groves, all seem of a piece.

That in mind, I was drawn to an article in the July 2003 issue of *Harper's* magazine and grew increasingly animated as I read it, for it seemed so close in its entire outlook to the book I was writing, the one you hold in your hands. Titled "A Gospel According to the Earth," the piece by contributing editor Jack Hitt notes the decline of organized religion in the United States ("the number of people identifying themselves as Christian is dropping one per cent per year") and the rise of what he called "eco-faith." The fifteen-page article was adorned by pastoral illustrations and the kind of vividly coloured tree-of-life embellishment in the margins one sees in illuminated texts from the Middle Ages.

Hitt sees environmentalism as a powerful new form of paganism—not "a set of nice feelings about land and animals" but "a rival to the power religion has held in people's lives." What had triggered his rumination, in part, was a visit to a friend's cabin in the woods of Appalachia, where the owner lived off the grid and grew his own food. The man talked about growing vegetables in compost, in a manner prescribed by Rudolph Steiner and involving ritualistic burying of cow manure with bark and animal skull. The two men talked till dawn and, at one point, Hitt removed himself and frantically began taking notes. He found himself writing words such as *communion* and *transcendence* and *ceremony,* unable to "shake this small moment. I never again thought of environmentalism as a movement about the politics of the land without noticing how often there were about it inklings of the divine."

I begin to wonder if latter-day pantheism marks a return to something ancient, something that predates Christianity and organized religion. When the Carthusian monks say "Never less alone than when alone" or when Rachel Carson writes (in *The Sense of Wonder*) that "those who dwell, as scientists or laymen, among the beauties and mysteries of the earth are never alone or weary of life," I hear them to echo what the Dakota Sioux have always believed: that there is no such thing as solitude. In his book *My People the Sioux,* published in 1928, Luther Standing

Bear wrote that Sioux elders taught their children to trust—and talk to—the land, the animals, and the forces of nature as they would members of their own family. The vision quest undertaken at puberty by Dakota boys—who would spend days alone, naked and fasting in the mountains—was meant to put them in touch with the animal-spirit guardians fated for them. I have yet to fast or walk naked at the cabin, but there is no doubt—in my mind at least—that the cabin puts me a little closer to what Dakota elders had in mind when they filled a sacred pipe with tobacco and prayed that a boy's journey might succeed, that "he may be one with the four winds, the four Powers of the world, and with the light of the dawn."

A cousin of mine works for the Ministry of Natural Resources in Fort Frances, where Ontario, Manitoba, and Minnesota intersect at Canada's virtual centre. It's lake and cabin country, not cottage country. (Though some people up there, as they do elsewhere in Canada, call their rustic retreats "camps.") "Almost everybody up here," my cousin tells me, "has a cabin. Some of these places have been in the same family for generations. It's like holy ground."

That remark piqued my curiosity and led me to seek out a few of the locals, such as Patti Collett, who would help me understand the depth of feeling that long-held cabins can engender. Patti's own cabin has been a family meeting ground for almost forty years. About a decade ago, Patti's niece sent her a piece of "descriptive writing" for a high school project. "She sent it to me in the mail," says Patti, "and as I started to read it I was a bit confused as to what it was about. When I reached the fourth line I started to cry as I realized she was writing about our cabin."

Though the writing was awkward in places, it was compelling, too. The niece, the then teenage Julia Cohen, had captured details of the cabin—"the bumpy stone path" that leads to it and "the small, untamed trees and thistles" along the way, the books on shelves inside the cabin (by Jack London, Ernest Hemingway, old how-to books and religious texts), the vintage baseball cards (one of Mickey Mantle). But more than the texture, she had caught the magic of the place and her own feeling for it.

"The cabin looks its years," Julia wrote. "Its roof sags slightly, the porch railing is broken in places, the windows are dull grey from the passage of time. Yet somehow, its aesthetics are reassuring ... The inside of the cabin smells of wood and breathes of life. It consists of one room that is kitchen, living and dining room all in one. A bedroom and bathroom lead off of it. Plywood lies on top of the rafters near the ceiling to provide a private hideaway for children ... Soft beige curtains, once white, filter the bright light from outdoors until it is as soft as a child's touch." Julia felt in the cabin "the echoes of lives lived" and observed that "its aura is such that once you are upon it, you feel ... you are at home."

Patti Collett is quite certain that her place is a *cabin,* one defined by its simplicity and unpretentiousness. Around Fort Frances, a *cottage* implies fancier notions—carpeting and indoor plumbing. A *camp* suggests tourists and rental units. Patti's little cabin at Rocky Inlet, on Rainy Lake, started as a "motor shack" on the water—a shed for boat motors, life jackets, and fuel cans, but with a loft for sleeping and a pot-bellied stove. Then came the cabin, with windows from an old schoolhouse and chipboard siding. "Dad did everything himself," says Patti. "Nothing is square," and she laughs aloud at the thought.

The odd thing about Patti's cabin is that she and her husband bought the place in 1983 and later built their house on the one-acre property. Cabin and house are only a minute apart. But some nights they'll walk down to the water and decide to sleep in the cabin where they are transported by smell (of must and mouse, of earth and wood) and memory (the piece of driftwood Patti's father painted and decorated with fish hooks, presents from boaters rescued on the lake, every piece of furniture with a story to tell).

"It's a whole different world at the cabin," Patti says, "but it's not the Hilton and it's not for everyone. Some people—like your cousin, who bunked at the cabin for a month—walk in and say 'Oh my God, this is fantastic.' There's nothing like being there."

Rena Upitis felt she was home the first time she saw the wide meadow that is the gateway to an imposing 204-acre piece of land north of Kingston that she bought in 1990. She was coming off a disastrous event in her life (an ill-advised marriage in Africa that had lasted three months) and she was at low ebb.

"I *love* this land, it's everything to me," she was saying one day in May as we marched about a mile to her cabin, past the beaver ponds, up steep and rocky inclines, along trails through hardwood forest where the Dutchman's breeches and trilliums were so stunning that sun-splashed day they made us forget the hard winter just past.

"I was looking for rugged, complicated land," she said, explaining her purchase. "I had always enjoyed the natural world and I was looking for land to steward, land to care for me." Rena was convinced that wilderness would somehow heal the deep wounds she then felt.

The forty-four-year-old woman ahead of me on that trail seemed part mountain goat. There was a little skip in her walk and the steeper the slope, the jauntier her gait, the bear bell at her hip ringing happily. With her short blond hair and blue eyes, her outback felt hat canted slightly back on her head, she looked as comfortable in those woods as a rider on an old and trusted horse.

Her features are soft, her frame a tad buttery, but they belie her fitness: the land that healed her has also made her strong. Rena has made a point of *not* putting a road in to her cabin, so naturally on this day she carries ten-foot-long two-by-fours on her shoulder and a pack on her back. Later, she asks if I'd like to take "the cliff trail" back to the truck for another load of lumber. Excuse me, I thought, I could have sworn we did a few cliffs on the way in.

Rena, you're thinking, is eccentric. And she would admit to that, perhaps with some pride. She is also a wife and the mother of two children, Hayden and Zinta, aged five and two-and-a-half. She is an artist (watercolour, acrylic, mixed media, clay, silk) and a musician (piano, cello, voice). And she was, for five years, dean of education at Queen's University before stepping down to become a professor of arts education. Rena has a doctorate in human development from Harvard University, she's crackerjack smart, but that day in 1990 as she followed up on a classified ad in the *Whig-Standard*—"Land For Sale"—she was pondering what it really means to be educated. In time she would come to believe that her basic education should include knowing how to build a little cabin on land you call your own. She paid $84,000 for that land, which works out to $412 an acre. I call that a bargain.

Picture her cabin. It sits on a rocky, treed outcrop overlooking a lake some twenty acres in size, a clear and ancient trout-filled lake ninety feet deep in the centre. Paddy's Lake is named after the Irishman who tried to farm this land in the late nineteenth century. A little timothy in the meadow is all that remembers Paddy Nolan's brave and foolhardy try; no trace remains of his log house high on the hill. There is only one other cabin on the lake, and while it's a fairly splendid counter to Rena's hermitage, its owner shares her green notions. "We're snobs," Rena laughs. Eco-snobs. The neighbour—a farmer and geographer named David who did graduate work on land reform—panicked when he saw that someone had bought the land across the water, then breathed a huge sigh of relief when he met Rena. "He got me," says Rena, "and I got him."

We sat on her cedar deck in Adirondack chairs, drinking herbal tea, admiring the loon across the way, listening to the riffle of wind through the trees and the woodpeckers in the far off, my eyes set on the high cliff across the lake. It's crown land over there, so Rena's peace seems—for the moment, anyway—unassailable. The United Nations has declared this land part of its biosphere program, land to be protected. And the *New York Times* (who told them?) put this topography on its list of the ten best places to buy land in North America. "This is heaven," I told Rena, "and I didn't even have to die to get here."

The wide and roomy privy, a short walk down the slope, is closed on three sides only and begs the user to choose views—the lake to the left, a sprawling marsh to the right. Talk about nature calling.

The cabin is modest in size (sixteen feet by twenty feet), with a ladder leading to a little loft at the south end. There is no electricity (though the plan is for solar power one day) and water comes from a small hand pump at the sink hooked up to a rain barrel outside. Every item in the cabin—the tables and chairs and little wooden wall cabinets, the twin propane tanks outside for the small fridge tucked inside one of the mouseproof cupboards, the board-and-batten pine that sheaths the exterior, the two woodstoves, windows, doors—all this was either brought in along the trail or rafted over from David's place. And lest you think the raft option is a breeze, consider that both cabins sit on promontories. Ever tried to move a woodstove across a room, never mind up or down a rocky incline? I imagined ropes and boards and rollers, teams of sweating men using trees as leverage, progress measured in inches. Like ants moving the rubber tree in that old song or the pyramid builders of ancient Egypt, the movers would have needed equal parts optimism and savvy. One of the stoves, I should say, is a small cook stove, but big enough to accommodate the turkey for the annual New Year's Day family and friends dinner at the cabin.

I thought of Adam Smith's old dictum, the one he wrote in *Wealth of Nations* in 1776: "The real price of every thing, what every thing really costs to the man who wants to acquire it, is the toil and trouble of acquiring it." By that reckoning, Rena's tiny cabin is a priceless castle.

She had help, of course. The crew would include her husband, Gary Rasberry—a musician and impresario—plus friends and high school students there to learn about building in the wilderness. But Rena, who had joined the building crew when the old schoolhouse in Yarker was gutted in 1984 and renovated to become their splendid house, had learned a thing or two about construction. About batter boards and building tubes, about plumb, level, and square. She designed her cabin, got the design approved, and either supervised a crew or worked alone as the cabin took shape in 1993. She still has the building inspector's report (he paddled over in a canoe), his blessing proudly displayed in a scrapbook called "Beating Around the Bush." Every co-op student got one and had contributed to it.

Some were "troubled" kids, some were former music students of Rena's, some just signed on as part of a work placement requirement at their high school in Kingston. One teenager jotted down this job description in the scrapbook: "dishwasher, trailblazer, furniture maker, pond duty supervisor, cook, bridge-maker ..." Rena was thinking that the placements would be all at once free labour, more fun for her than working alone, and a meaningful experience for them all. And she was right on every count.

One student, sixteen-year-old Andrea, observed that "Packing up is so sad. Well, back to civilization. Sniff, sniff. I'll miss the vibrant green, the sky against the living leaves, the smell of the fresh air, the lake at night, the sounds of animals ... it's been quite a week to say the least." They slept in tents, worked like dogs, gathered at the campfire every night. Years later, many of them have returned to visit, to see what's become of this cherished place.

"Here," says Rena, "I feel part of a bigger thing. The bigger thing is the pattern." To illustrate, she recalled a line from a poem about a "leaf not lost," how it knows its place in the forest. Rena on this land, in that cabin, feels very much at home.

Telling, too, is that three of Rena's women friends, all of them writers who have come often to the cabin in years past, have now built or had built cabins of their own. It takes a certain person, says Rena, to hike a hard mile for a bit of leisure and meditation. And while it may say something about the nature of Rena's pals, it also says something of this place that most visitors either proclaim it paradise or feel inspired to carve out their own little slice of heaven.

What is it that drives this cabin fever? I mentioned in a letter to a friend on Vancouver Island that I was writing a cabin book, and Star wrote back that she has a little writer's shack up the mountain. I asked Tom, a carpenter friend in Kingston, if he'd help me build a porch on my cabin and he said he'd love to, but he's embarking on a cabin of his own on his folks' cottage property in northwestern Ontario. My pal David has bought a house on a twelve-acre piece of land in Prince Edward County, and he took me to a high meadow where we feng-shuied around. He, too, has cabin dreams.

Meanwhile, a television commercial was recently pitching a luxury Ford SUV by first posting these words: "Luxury is a cabin in the woods"—then showing a polished black vehicle pulling up in front of a sprawling cabin in a forest clearing. The same car company later used a log house as a backdrop in another commercial for SUVs—one model called Explorer, another called Escape.

"A Magical Escape," read the headline of a travel piece in the *National Post* of December 21, 2002. The destination? Remote cabins in the snow-covered Rockies at Skoki Lodge, accessible only by hiking and horseback in summer, by cross-country skis and snowshoes in winter. The cabins and main lodge were built in 1932 from hand-cut pine logs; guests (no more than twenty-two can be accommodated at any one time) pay about $150 a night for the privilege of bunking there—despite, though more likely because of, no running water (outhouses for toilets), hurricane lamps for lights, and tilted floors. The author of the travel piece spent Christmas in a cabin there and found the rustic setup at the lodge enchanting, the views spellbinding ("like something out of Heidi's Switzerland"), the whole experience calming and nostalgic. The smell of gingerbread, stockings hung by the fire, candles on the Christmas tree, the crisp mountain air—the details seemed lifted from an old and familiar carol. Hiking the seven miles back to Lake Louise, the scribe was annoyed by lineups and "tinny rock music coming through loudspeakers"—like something from "another world." Implicit is the longing for that other, quieter, Heidi world, for the cabin retreat.

A modest cabin survey, but there you have it. And maybe my survey says something of my friends, or the age of my friends, or boomer demographics shaping advertising and editorial thinking—though there is no denying this longing for a little place tucked away. As we walked his place in the county, I suggested to David that he consider a certain spot by the woods near the ridge, a spot in the high southeast corner of the meadow where the west wind will have gathered enough momentum scooting across the field to drive off the mosquitoes, where the stand of shagbark hickory could shade his retreat. Best camp there first, I urged him. Get the feel of the place.

That's what Rena Upitis did before she chose her lookout. Similarly, she took two years pondering where to build the guest cabin. The day I was there she showed me the newly dug footings where that cabin will go, on a flat overlooking the marsh. "The Parthenon," she has dubbed it, after lugging twelve bags of cement along the trail. Twelve bags, twelve trips. Ever lifted a bag of cement? Rena long ago asked herself if she could build a cabin in the woods. "I'm smart! I'm strong," she answered herself, practically beating her chest as she relived that private conversation for my benefit. Smart and strong indeed.

With her that day, and on virtually all of her nigh weekly visitations to the cabin every month of the year, was her seven-year-old dog, Maggie. A mix of shepherd, retriever, and border collie, she is Rena's quiet and loyal companion on these treks. Zinta and Hayden come often, too, along with Gary—though he doesn't love the place "in his bones" as Rena does. So often she goes with only Maggie as company, and sometimes, knowing her need, Gary will suggest she go.

Having this land, Rena says, must be like having a lover. She knows it will take work to balance that love with her other loves—family, work, friends. But she also knows that her love for this land is "so strong, so deep. It's not negotiable."

Rena's land has become her sacred duty. Last year, an interesting job came up in the States, but Rena couldn't contemplate the move. "It wasn't that I couldn't leave our house in Yarker or beloved friends," she says. "It was the land. I couldn't leave the land." When I asked her to list the ten things she loves most about the cabin and the land it sits on, her How Do I Love Thee list went like this:

1. Solitude.
2. The air.
3. The trees.
4. The feel of walking in that cabin door and being "enveloped."
5. The personal history of the place and all its objects (the door with the brass buttressing from a Royal Military College dorm, the leaded glass window from the Beaches Public Library in Toronto, the "twig furniture" couch she made herself of willow and maple boughs and branches and where she has nursed her infants looking out at the lake).
6. Said lake "in all its manifestations."
7. The animals and birds.
8. The space—"the volume, the 3-D space, the openness of it all."
9. The wildness—"its unpredictability, its mutability. Something new has grown, something is gone, something is frightening. It's all a gift."
10. The weather. "Here there is no bad weather. I can get warm here (throw another log on the fire), I can get cool here (jump in the lake)."

The hermitage is not without its scourges, of course. The blackflies were taking the measure of us that day and the mosquitoes, horseflies, and deer flies had yet to form their squadrons. Rena's wearing of the bear bell followed her sighting last year of a great pile of bear scat on one of the trails. In winter, she cannot get her truck onto the rough road that leads to the meadow, and snowshoeing in takes one and a half hours on good days, more than four hours on bad ones. One winter night at the cabin (this was before she insulated the place), it was minus twenty-eight degrees *inside* the cabin. The pee in her antique commode had turned to ice, her blankets were stiff as boards, her eyelashes were frozen to her face, and the propane stove wouldn't light.

One day recently, when Rena was at the cabin with her two young children, she called for them and neither answered. Each had wandered down one of the twenty trails on the property—the north trail, the stream trail, the cliff trail. Heart in mouth, she found each child and managed to stifle her own panic while donning her childhood educator's hat. First she asked them to tell Mama what they had seen on the trail; *then* she reminded them of the rule about never going off alone into the forest. Rena felt the fear that pioneer mothers must have felt, but she also felt a surge of pride—her young children had the confidence, the curiosity to go exploring in the woods that will one day be theirs.

I wanted to know from Rena Upitis what it was in her past, in her makeup, that allowed such tree-huggery to flourish. "I come," she said, "from a long line of land lovers. My culture is Latvian, and Latvian culture is pagan." Rena's mother grew up in the Lutheran church but taught Rena as well about the natural, and largely female, deities—the sacred sun (*saule,* pronounced *sow*-le), the moon and stars, trees and snakes and toads, fire and water.

Rena's family in Latvia tend to live in tiny city apartments while owning tracts of land outside the capital city of Riga. "Being on land is all I heard about. There is this eternal feeling," she says, "as if these are the conversations my family has had for generations and I just joined in." Rena had grown up in Port Coquitlam, British Columbia, a tomboy who built tree forts and wept at the loss of them when the family moved to suburban Calgary when she was thirteen. The cabin, she admits, has its roots in those tree forts.

When Rena and Gary got married in 1995, they were married at the cabin. The white straw hat with trailing yellow ribbon she wore that day hangs on the wall at the cabin as a memento. The 120 guests braved the trail, with the elderly ferried over on the raft. When the rain came, warm August rain but a downpour nonetheless, some guests were driven away but sixty-four sheltered in that little cabin, the kids crammed into the loft, and eight guests gathered in the privy (where they were served champagne in fluted crystal glasses). Rena has a vivid memory of her Latvian aunts and uncles, standing in the rain while wearing garbage bags and saying they couldn't wait to go home and tell friends how people get married in Canada.

Some guests tucked in under the tool shed roof. Rena had built the shed the week before the wedding to house folding chairs. It rained then, too, so she worked naked but for steel-toed boots and a tool belt at her waist. She and Gary were a week preparing for the wedding—building steps on the trail, hauling in food and china.

Rena finds, as I do, salvation in toil. "Here I work," she says, beaming with the notion. "I feel a surge of energy here. I'm not frantic. It's about making things with your hands. The physical part of it is massive, and the satisfaction from physical work is not something many people get."

When the cabin was more or less built, it was time for the adornments, the little touches that made it feel like home. Some items were lugged in even before the concrete was poured. One of the first things Rena carried in was a piece of pottery she had made—a fish that hangs on the east wall. There is also, and this I found completely incongruous, a loudly ticking wall clock. "No noise is permitted at the cabin," says Rena (and thus the silent propane fridge), but she found the quiet *too* profound and introduced the ticking clock whose sound she finds rhythmical, even musical. On the walls are several long strips of bevelled glass, samples from a glass manufacturer in Kingston, that cast intriguing light and reflections. There are also, above the sink, many shiny baking tins and salad moulds with candles attached (by metal pegs, in the manner of German Christmas trees). "On a winter's night, the light from them," she says, "is *amazing*. It's like a fairy tale." There is an old Underwood typewriter Rena uses to write poetry and research papers. A flying frog hangs on a thread from the ceiling, for good luck.

This is Rena's *cabin*. It is no *cottage*. For her, the cottage is about recreation, and she means by that the usual notion of boating, waterskiing, and fishing but also recreating what one has at home—dishwasher, television, mod cons. The cottage, she believes, insulates you from the natural world. The cabin, or at least her notion of the cabin, is about bringing earth and earthling a little closer together.

One night at the cabin, Rena had a dream, though nightmare is more like it, for the dream was about Paradise Lost. Across the lake she saw a cottage subdivision rising, with docks and boats, motorboats everywhere. She awoke, dripping wet, but when she looked out across Paddy's Lake, the pristine cliff was still there in the light of the moon, as were the stands of conifer and birch. It would soon be dawn and *saule* would rise over the lake. Rena would get to work—planting her woodland garden, building the Parthenon, with maybe time in the afternoon for a cup of tea and a rest in the swinging hammock below the pines. Another day at the cabin, another good day.

EPILOGUE

Several months after writing a long essay for the *Ottawa Citizen* on the cabin's resurrection, I happened to chat once more with that newspaper's features editor. "You know," he said, mildly baffled, "people still talk about that article. It struck some sort of chord." Perhaps my goofy apprenticeship had taught me, and the reader, something useful.

Maybe the cabin and places like it answer some fundamental need. Leonard Cohen gave an interview a few years ago in which he described how his lifelong depression had mysteriously vanished. The lifting of this scourge followed years in a monastery in California where his life was highly ritualized and blissfully simple, built around menial labour and time alone in nature.

Some 80 per cent of Canadians now live in cities where many spend hours commuting to work, shopping in underground malls, living and working in high-rise buildings. Such a life is almost completely disconnected from the earth, the seasons, the natural world with all its sounds and wonders.

As for the land beyond the cities, much of it is owned by farmers, and many farmers are in trouble. In her book *Another Season's Promise: Hope and Despair in Canada's Farm Country,* the Winnipeg author Ingeborg Boyens notes, for example, that each year some fifty million kilograms (one hundred and ten million pounds) of herbicides, fungicides, and pesticides are sprayed on Canadian soil; such sprays constitute the farmer's single greatest operating expense. Factor in uneven government subsidies and the hardball tactics of agribusiness, and it becomes easier to understand why many Canadian farmers make no profit at all. Something is terribly wrong with this picture, and has been for decades.

Unmanageable scale is another problem. Hog, cattle, and chicken waste from ever grander factory farms inevitably heightens the risk of groundwater contamination. The corporate farm, like any corporation, is inclined to grow, swallow competitors, and carve out a monopoly. It seeks integration so that grain producer and bread producer—to cite just one example—become one. None of this is good news for either the farmer or the land.

Many reasons exist for rethinking. First, farmers can ill afford the cost of sprays; there is also the wider cost of chemicals—yet to be truly tabulated—to the environment and human health. Second, a small tide has turned in favour of organic food, with that market growing by up to 25 per cent each year. And finally, the *price* of food is not the only form of accounting; *quality* of food, the plight of animals raised in dark chutes, the social fabric of small places—all this, says Boyens, must count for something. Or does it? Unless the current course is altered, the family farm will go on giving way to huge corporate farms—with today's farmers mere serfs on land they once owned. The solution, or part of it, may be as simple as going for a walk.

Sharon Butala in *The Perfection of the Morning: An Apprenticeship in Nature* talks about "building a relationship with nature"—by walking her land and paying attention to what she sees. Soren Kierkegaard, the nineteenth-century Danish philosopher and theologian, once advised a friend in a letter, "Above all, do not lose your desire to walk: every day I walk myself into a state of well-being and walk away from every illness; I have walked myself into my best thoughts, and I know of no thought so burdensome that one cannot walk away from it ... the more one sits still, the closer one comes to feeling ill ... if one just keeps on walking, everything will be all right."

If walking is good for the soul, perhaps walking your own land is even better. Imagine this scenario. Let's say that a farmer with one thousand acres sells two or three hundred acres to a city family seeking a foot in both camps—the urban and the rural.

What if that parcel were to be shared, giving a city family a stake in the country and the farmer some needed cash plus some use of the land? My own situation is not unusual. Though I would prefer to spend most of, if not all, my time at the cabin, that's not possible for the moment and might never come to pass. In the meantime, my arrangement with the farmer who works our land suits both of us. Farmer Guernsey gets the use of three ten-acre fields at no cost; my only condition is that he avoid using chemical sprays. I'm not sure he's pleased by my nudging him toward organic farming, but he does it nonetheless. His working the fields not only controls weeds in the meadows (sparing me the trouble), but offers me the aesthetic satisfaction that comes with a field of wheat or hay swaying in the breezes. It's a mutually satisfying arrangement, one that ideally assigns two stewards to the land.

Not everyone can afford to buy land, but many seem able to afford stocks (which are reeling as I write this). Actually, it's not that people have the luxury of buying shares, it is that both the federal government (by making RRSP-eligible shares tax deductible) and the mutual fund industry (by its fear mongering about geriatric destitution) make it seem a wise and even inevitable course of action. Many people have become convinced that the Canada Pension Plan will be bankrupt by the time baby boomers want to access it, but the ones yelling most loudly that the sky is falling also sell shares. Now and then, saner voices are heard to offer other possibilities. To which I would add this one: if and when the house gets paid off, or a small windfall or inheritance comes your way, why not put a few thousand down on a woodlot?

Now spread that idea across the country. City folk, town folk—some of them tenants all their lives—would suddenly become *land* lords. Maybe just a few acres on a quiet river, a ten-acre parcel on the Canadian Shield, a hundred acres of tired pasture. (As a rule, the bigger the parcel, the cheaper the cost per acre.)

Farmers, long used to renting land from other farmers, would henceforth do at least some business with urban folk. No doubt some of these land use arrangements would have to be formalized, but maybe not. A handshake once did the job; maybe that custom could be revived.

Now take land ownership a step further, toward land stewardship. Land conservation agreements can protect a piece of land from any unwanted development—mining, logging, building—well into the future. Some covenants can be imposed on that land and all who will own it "forever." The Nature Conservancy of Canada, for example, is entitled to execute conservation agreements.

The Nature Conservancy—by direct purchase of land, by gifts of land or conservation agreements with owners—has protected some 1.8 million acres of land in Canada. The short-term downside to land conservation agreements (though it looks long-term upside to me) is that imposing restrictive covenants on land effectively lowers its value as real estate, so what happens is this. A specially trained appraiser determines what the land was worth before the convenants were applied. Let's say that land once worth fifty thousand dollars is now deemed to be worth thirty-five thousand dollars; this means that the potential value of your agreement—your "eco-gift"—is up to fifteen thousand dollars. Where the land is of exceptional merit (habitat to rare species of plant or animal), the landowner may be entitled to a deduction approaching fifteen thousand dollars. The eco-gift may trigger a capital gains tax and the net tax benefit will be different in each case, depending on your personal tax situation.

Those without land and struggling to afford the purchase price could get a little closer to owning land by first buying it, agreeing to protect it, and then using the charitable tax deduction to offset the purchase price.

So, city folk to the rescue, not just of the family farm, but to their own rescue. Land could be saved, piece by piece, acre by acre, tract by tract, and I'm betting that each landowner would be the better for it.

I wonder, too, if private land could serve the public good. All across this country, hobby farmers and absentee landowners rent out their arable land to willing farmers or let it lie fallow. On several occasions, the farmer who uses our land has planted a crop and sold it to raise money for one of his church's charities. What if other landowners were to do the same? Should some of us be planting potatoes for food banks? What about flowers?

Friends who live in the country, Jane and Peter Good, dedicate one entire acre to an annual flower garden—the sunflowers rising to my chest midsummer, the size of the garden almost beyond imagining—and every week Jane delivers flowers to the local hospice day program in Kingston (where she works at the university). Flora Vita, she calls it, flowers for life. At an annual event, about a hundred of her friends and friends of friends come to their farm over the course of several weekends, clipping flowers to our hearts' content, tossing donations into a jar, and taking home our stunning bouquets. Proceeds go to hospice and nonprofit palliative care. The hobby farm put to noble use.

Well into the writing of this book, I chanced across Aldo Leopold's *A Sand County Almanac*—published in 1949, the year

I was born. Somehow, I had missed this little gem that only found its readership in the environmental salad days of the 1960s, when it sold a million copies. What has endured is Leopold's notion of a "land ethic"—his belief that government agencies can only do so much to protect the land, that it falls to each landowner and his or her own "ecological conscience."

Aldo Leopold was a man of science with the heart of a poet. In 1935 he bought, for a song, an abandoned farm—120 acres of land in the so-called sand counties of central Wisconsin along with a cowshed he would henceforth call "the shack." His first act was to plant a food patch for wildlife; the Leopolds—Aldo, his wife, Estella, and their five children—would go on planting: prairie grasses, wildflowers, shrubs, and trees (up to six thousand pines every spring!). The lesson of Aldo Leopold is this: To know the land is to love it.

Here's Susan Flader, a professor of environmental history at the University of Missouri-Columbia: "For Leopold and his family," she wrote in her essay in *Companion to A Sand County Almanac* in 1987, "the shack years were an experience in the slow sensitizing of people to land, the evolution of a sense of country." The shack originally acquired as a hunting camp soon became "a weekend refuge from too much modernity," a place to hike and swim and breathe the good air, to build by hand, to split wood and bake sourdough bread, to sing and talk and laugh into the night.

And the more woodcocks and chickadees and nuthatches the Leopolds saw, the more they planted vegetation that met those birds' needs. "In short," Flader wrote, "the more familiar they became with the place—the more they found to anticipate, to ponder, to marvel at." Leopold was transforming the land with all his planting, but it went the other way, too. The land was transforming him.

Leopold believed that if you spend enough time on a particular piece of land, sit quietly, listen hard, and think of all you have seen and tried to fathom, "then you may hear it—a vast pulsing harmony—its score inscribed on a thousand hills, its notes the lives and deaths of plants and animals, its rhythms spanning the seconds and the centuries."

In the foreword to his book, written just a month before he died, Aldo Leopold wrote, "There are some who can live without wild things and some who cannot. These essays are the delights and dilemmas of one who cannot." Later, speaking for his family, he added that on their land "we seek—and still find—our meat from God."

What was special about Leopold was his belief—then, as now, heretical in some quarters—that we abuse land and treat it as a commodity because we are detached from it, see it as just another possession. But as we cozy up over time with one topography, seeing ourselves as linked to all that lives there, something happens. E.O. Wilson makes the same point in *Biophilia,* when he quotes a German expert on the honeybee, which he likened to "a magic well: the more you draw from it, the more there is to draw." Wilson believes that if each of us were to become a naturalist in our own backyard—however small or large those yards might be—we would feel again the thrill that a child feels.

Leopold took the long view, for he was, at heart, an optimist. In 1947, he observed that it had taken nineteen centuries to define decent man-to-man conduct and that the process remained only half finished. "It may take as long," he added, "to evolve a code of decency for man-to-land conduct." Falling for land, as Leopold saw it, is a process, a quest, by turns personal, religious, scientific. He always walked his refuge with a notebook in which he recorded the early blooms of pitcher plants, the numbers of geese arriving, mammal sightings in the woods. The day he died (of a coronary while fighting a neighbour's grass-fire), he had a notebook in his pocket. The last line read, "lilac shoots 2" long."

Leopold did not rank beauty, but took it as he saw it. A snow-covered mountain in a national park was no more to be admired, and no less, than his own pond or meadow. The difference was that he knew that pond's story, for he had seen it unfolding for decades. He had brought to his land a quiet eye, and his harvest included his inspirational almanac, many thousands of tall pines, and much else.

Near the end of *The Perfection of the Morning,* Sharon Butala describes a conversation she once had with an old man who had farmed and raised cattle on the prairie all his life. They were talking (and this was years before her book was published in 1994) about the financial ruin that faced many farmers and how Saskatchewan was losing its population. The old man said he was sure that one day there would be people on every quarter section, as there had been when he was a boy. When Butala asked him how that might transpire, he looked off into the distance and simply restated his conviction. "I couldn't forget what he'd said," Butala wrote, "because it seemed so clearly a visionary moment to me, beyond reason, beyond the facts. I thought he had seen something that was more than a dream ..."

I like to think his dream has legs, not like the dreams of the vanquished Blackfoot chiefs who tried desperately to dance the buffalo back into existence. The novelist Wallace Stegner once observed that "something will have gone out of us as a people if we ever let the remaining wilderness be destroyed." He was urging as far back as 1960 a "wilderness bank" and "a geography of hope." Aldo Leopold would have concurred. "Of what avail are forty freedoms," he wrote, "without a blank space on the map?"

The cabin is my place in the sun, though I fear the sun and give it wide berth when I can. For the sun may be the death of me, and the cabin a part of what I leave behind. "Old man Scanlan built that cabin," a neighbour may one day say. "Bit of a pioneer nut, but he sure loved that place. Even wrote a book about it."

When I was a boy, a freckled lad with Irish blood coursing in me from both sides, I took it as a given that I would suffer sunburns all summer long. I would burn through cotton jerseys, blisters would rise like tapioca on my neck and arms. Along with carsickness and shyness, sunburn-ness was my lot in life, and I accepted it. Foolishly, recklessly, I would later join my teenage friends basking on lakeshore beaches and by swimming pools, hoping the freckles might somehow band together and form that always elusive tan. The freckles never cooperated. That night I would be forced to sleep in a jury-rigged tent—sheets held up on either side of me by bookbinders, sheets to keep off the night chill but kept aloft, for I could bear no contact. My flesh those nights was a vibrant pink where the sun had done its work, white as bleached bone elsewhere, and the lines between the two zones were sharp. I remember the smell of vinegar and calamine lotion and the goosebumps rising as my mother put on these salves, as delicately as she could. I remember standing in the kitchen in my underwear, wondering how I could feel so hot and so cold at the same time.

In my late forties, there was a reckoning. My family doctor saw little of me, for I was otherwise healthy, but I would develop more than a nodding acquaintance with my dermatologist and the surgeons he would send me to. I remember what the doctor said the first time the biopsy came back positive. "You've got a bit of cancer," he said on the telephone.

The phrase seemed alarming yet comforting. I didn't *have* cancer, I had a touch of it. There was the prospect that it would go away with a hack and a snip, and, if it returned, we would keep cutting. No radiation, no chemotherapy, not yet, anyway, and even the surgery was of the outpatient variety. There were worse forms of the disease. My mother, my mother's brother, my father's sister, many of my friends had gone down that road and never come back, so I was grateful—and still, not a little terrified.

I tell the story as warning, as public service. Do not take the sun lightly, especially if your skin is light. Wear a wide-brimmed hat in the sun, cover up. My lesions have occurred on my face, my left ear, my left arm—perhaps from decades of the sun hitting that side of me as I drove. So, take heed. Take to the shade.

In another way, the lesions have been a blessing. It must be what a soldier feels when a mortar goes off close to him, and, though sprayed with stones and dirt and rocked to his core, he is surprised and delighted to be alive. For a while longer, anyway.

If the cabin is where I go to breathe, it is also the place where I feel most alive. When I "pass" (the favoured verb of Doris, the obit writer at the newspaper in British Columbia that once employed the two of us), the cabin and environs is the place I will miss most. I fell in love with that land the moment we broke the soil and started raising those old Bresee timbers. I like to think we will leave a little mark there, a pleasing and unusual addition to the landscape, one that gave me grief and then more peace and contentment than I had ever known.

Ask me and I will tell you. If you can, buy a little land, build something, a modest cabin, say, and build it well, with care and imagination and as much daring as you can. Go there alone, or with others, walk that land often and make a spring ritual of planting trees there. Cherish that land, learn its past and safeguard its future. Come to knows its rhythms. A dog may not be essential to complete the picture, but if you ask me I will tell you that a dog most certainly is. May your cabin be a quiet place, may it have a porch and a rocker, may it please you and all who go there. This book was written in praise of the plain and simple sanctuary, and I hope you have one or might consider seeking one.

And do give your place in the sun a name. "Larry's Folly," I'm afraid, is taken.

ACKNOWLEDGMENTS

Several people read early versions of this book and had a hand in shaping it. I am most grateful to Ulrike Bender, J.D. Carpenter, Charlotte Gray, Janet Lunn, Marilyn Smith, Jamie Swift, and Rena Upitis. My agent, Jackie Kaiser, has her own cabin dreams and did much to nurture this one.

I thank Anna Bresee for her letters and memories, Robert Gregoire for his kindness and expertise, Sandy MacLachlan for his time and passion, Rolf Vassbotn for deciphering and defending the building code, Michael Keeling for building with such care (Peter Blendell and Robert Wiens likewise). The Archives and Collection Society in Picton proved a most useful resource and I spent several happy days there exploring the history of Prince Edward County.

All at Penguin (my editor, Diane Turbide, especially) supported the project at every turn and made the work a pleasure, as did copy editor Sarah Weber.

Family and friends—too numerous to name—have all helped in their way to foster both the cabin and the book it spawned. For picking rocks and digging holes, for planting trees and building beds, for painting walls and doors, for your castoff furniture, for the photos you took and the genuine pleasure you take in the place—thanks to you all, and especially, and as always, to Oma and Opa and Pop, to Ulrike and Kurt.

Bibliography

Abrahamson, Una. *God Bless Our Home: Domestic Life in Nineteenth Century Canada.* Toronto: Burns & MacEachern, 1966.

Alexander, Christopher, Sara Ishikawa, and Murray Silverstein with Max Jacobson, Ingrid Fiksdahl-King, and Shlomo Angel. *A Pattern Language: Towns, Buildings, Construction.* New York: Oxford University Press, 1977.

Bishop, Morris. *Champlain: The Life of Fortitude.* Toronto: McClelland & Stewart, 1963.

Boyens, Ingeborg. *Another Season's Promise: Hope and Despair in Canada's Farm Country.* Toronto: Penguin, 2001.

Brill, David. *A Separate Place: A Father's Reflections on Building a Home and Renewing a Family.* New York: Plume, 2000.

Burns, Max. *Cottage Water Systems.* Toronto: Cottage Life Books, 1995.

Butala, Sharon. *The Perfection of the Morning: An Apprenticeship in Nature.* Toronto: HarperCollins, 1994.

Callicott, J. Baird, ed. *Companion to A Sand County Almanac.* Madison, WI: University of Wisconsin Press, 1987.

Canniff, William. *The Settlement of Upper Canada.* Belleville, ON: Mika, 1971.

Carson, Rachel. *The Sense of Wonder.* New York: HarperCollins, 1956.

Chatwin, Bruce. *The Songlines.* New York: Viking, 1987.

Christopher, Peter, and Richard Skinulis. *Log Houses: Canadian Classics.* Erin, ON: Boston Mills, 1995.

Cohen, Matt. *Typing: A Life in 26 Keys.* Toronto: Random House, 2000.

Czajkowski, Chris. *Cabin at Singing River: Building a Home in the Wilderness.* Camden East, ON: Camden House, 1991.

Davidson, Laura Lee. *A Winter of Content.* New York: Abingdon Press, 1922.

Dillard, Annie. *For the Time Being.* Toronto: Viking, 1999.

———. *Pilgrim at Tinker Creek.* New York: Perennial, 1988.

Dodds, Philip F. *Athol: Stories of a Township and Its People During the Past 132 Years.* Athol, ON: Athol Township Senior Citizens' Activity Group, 1979.

Ehrenhaft, George. *The Builder's Secret: Learning the Art of Living Through the Craft of Building.* Rocklin, CA: Prima Publishing, 1999.

Ehrlich, Gretel. *The Solace of Open Spaces.* New York: Penguin, 1985.

Elledge, Scott. *E.B. White: A Biography.* New York: W.W. Norton, 1984.

Finnigan, Joan. *I Come from the Valley.* Toronto: NC Press, 1976.

Frayne, Jill. *Starting Out in the Afternoon: A Mid-Life Journey into Wild Land.* Toronto: Vintage, 2000.

Gilbert, Elizabeth. *The Last American Man.* New York: Penguin, 2002.

Gill, Ray, ed. *How to Build 20 Cabins*. New York: Arco, 1955.

Gray, Charlotte. *Sisters in the Wilderness: The Lives of Susanna Moodie and Catharine Parr Traill*. Toronto: Penguin, 1999.

Guillet, Edwin Clarence. *Early Life in Upper Canada*. Toronto: University of Toronto Press, 1969.

Head, George. *Forest Scenes and Incidents in the Wilds of North America; Being a Diary of a Winter's Route from Halifax to the Canadas, and During Four Months' Residence in the Woods on the Borders of Lakes Huron and Simcoe*. London: John Murray, 1829.

Henderson, Bill. *Tower: Faith, Vertigo, and Amateur Construction*. New York: Farrar, Straus and Giroux, 2000.

Hummel, Monte. *Wintergreen: Reflections on Loon Lake*. Toronto: Key Porter, 1999.

Kahn, Ashley. *Kind of Blue: The Making of the Miles Davis Masterpiece*. New York: Da Capo Press, 2000.

Kavaler, Lucy. *Noise: The New Menace*. New York: John Day, 1975.

Kidder, Tracy. *House*. Boston: Houghton Mifflin, 1985.

Knowles, Joseph. *Alone in the Wilderness*. Boston: Small, Maynard and Co., 1913.

Knudtson, Peter, and David Suzuki. *Wisdom of the Elders*. Toronto: Stoddart, 1992.

Laird, Ross A. *Grain of Truth: The Ancient Lessons of Craft*. Toronto: Macfarlane Walter & Ross, 2001.

Leopold, Aldo. *A Sand County Almanac*. New York: Oxford University Press, 1949.

Lunn, Richard, and Janet Lunn. *The County: The First Hundred Years in Loyalist Prince Edward*. Picton, ON: Prince Edward County Council, 1967.

MacDonald, Jake. *Houseboat Chronicles: Notes from a Life in Shield Country*. Toronto: McClelland & Stewart, 2002.

MacGregor, Roy. *Escape: In Search of the Natural Soul of Canada.* Toronto: McClelland & Stewart, 2002.

McRaven, Charles. *Building and Restoring the Hewn Log House.* Cincinatti: Betterway Books, 1994.

Moodie, Susanna. *Life in the Clearings.* Toronto: Macmillan, 1959.

———. *Roughing It in the Bush, or, Forest Life in Canada.* Toronto: McClelland & Stewart, 1923.

Moss, John. *Bellrock.* Toronto: NC Press, 1983.

Mulfinger, Dale, and Susan E. Davis. *The Cabin: Inspiration for the Classic American Getaway.* Newton, CT: Taunton Press, 2001.

Muir, John. *Our National Parks.* Boston: Houghton, Mifflin, 1901.

Nash, Roderick Frazier. *Wilderness and the American Mind.* New Haven, CT: Yale University Press, 2001

O'Brien, Flann. *The Third Policeman.* New York: Plume, 1967.

Powning, Beth. *Seeds of Another Summer: Finding the Spirit of Home in Nature.* Toronto: Penguin, 1996.

Prince Edward Historical Society. *Historic Prince Edward.* Picton, ON: Prince Edward Historical Society, 1966.

Redner, Douglas K. *It Happened in Prince Edward County.* Belleville, ON: Mika, 1976.

Richardson Jr., Robert D. *Henry David Thoreau: A Life of the Mind.* Berkeley, CA: University of California Press, 1986.

Rooke, Constance, ed. *Writing Home: A PEN Canada Anthology.* Toronto: McClelland & Stewart, 1997.

Rybczynski, Witold. *The Most Beautiful House in the World.* New York: Penguin, 1989.

Scanlan, Lawrence. *Heading Home: On Starting a New Life in a Country Place.* Toronto: Doubleday, 1996.

Schafer, R. Murray. *The Tuning of the World.* Toronto: McClelland & Stewart, 1977.

———. *Voices of Tyranny, Temples of Silence.* Indian River, ON: Arcana Editions, 1993.

Schama, Simon. *Landscape and Memory*. Toronto: Vintage, 1995.

Secrest, Meryle. *Frank Lloyd Wright: A Biography*. New York: Knopf, 1992.

Seib, Charles. *The Woods: One Man's Escape to Nature*. Garden City, NJ: Doubleday, 1971.

Siebert, Charles. *Wickerby: An Urban Pastoral*. New York: Crown, 1998.

Still, Henry. *In Quest of Quiet*. Harrisburg, PA: Stackpole Books, 1970.

Thayer, William Makepeace. *From Log-Cabin to White House*. London: Hodder, 1881.

Thoreau, Henry David. *Walden, or, Life in the Woods*. New York: C.N. Potter, 1970.

Tocqueville, Alexis de. *Democracy in America*. New York: Knopf, 1945.

Traill, Catharine Parr. *Canadian Crusoes*. Toronto: McClelland & Stewart, 1923.

———. *Lost in the Backwoods: A Tale of the Canadian Forest*. London: Nelson, 1882.

Turner, Frederick. *Beyond Geography: The Western Spirit Against the Wilderness*. New Brunswick, NJ: Rutgers University Press, 1992.

Weslager, Clinton Alfred. *The Log Cabin in America*. New Brunswick, NJ: Rutgers University Press, 1969.

Wharton, Edith. *Italian Villas and Their Gardens*. New York: Da Capo Press, 1976.

White, E.B. *Essays of E.B. White*. New York: Harper & Row, 1977.

Wilkins, Charles. *A Wilderness Called Home: Dispatches from the Wild Heart of Canada*. Toronto: Peguin, 2001.

Wilson, E.O. *Biophilia*. Cambridge, MA: Harvard University Press: 1984.

Wright, Frank Lloyd. *Testament*. New York: Bramhall House, 1957.